The New Testament

A Study Guide

Coy D. Roper

CYPRESS

Copyright © 2024 by Coy D. Roper

Cataloging-in-Publication Data

Roper, Coy D. (Coy Dee), 1937-2023

Notes on the New Testament / by Coy D. Roper

p. cm.

ISBN 978-1-956811-57-5 (hc) 978-1-956811-58-2 (ebook)1. Bible. New Testament—Introductions. 2. Bible. New Testament—Criticism, interpretation, etc. I. Author. II. Title.

225.61—dc20

Library of Congress Control Number: 2024935618

Cover design by Brad McKinnon and Brittany Vander Maas.

Cypress Publications
3625 Helton Drive
PO Box HCU
Florence, AL 35630

www.hcu.edu

To June Shannon

Christian Lady
Talented Teacher and Writer
Who Has Been to Me an Encourager and Helper
and Who Is the Mother of My Wonderful Wife

Contents

Introduction

For many years, the late Coy Roper taught Critical Introduction to the New Testament for Heritage Christian University. Notes on the New Testament is a collection of the notes he used to teach that popular and challenging course. In addition to chapters on the content, value, and authenticity of each New Testament book, Dr. Roper includes chapters on "Scriptures Related to the Inspiration of the New Testament," "Notes on the Canon of the New Testament," "The Textual Criticism of the New Testament," and "Suggestions Regarding Translations." Though some of the references show a bit of age, his respect for and understanding of the New Testament remains clear. So does his love of the God-given text. As one reads Notes on the New Testament, it's good to hear Dr. Roper's solid and pleasant voice again.

Bill Bagents

The New Testament

Scriptures Related to the Inspiration of the New Testament

2 TIMOTHY 3:16, 17; 2 PETER 1:20, 21; JOHN 10:35; Hebrews 1:1, 2 — The Old Testament scriptures were regarded as inspired and authoritative.

2 Peter 3:15, 16 — Peter spoke of Paul's writings as scripture. Therefore, Paul's writings were regarded as inspired and authoritative.

Matthew 28:18–20; Hebrews 1:1, 2 — Jesus spoke with all authority. He authoritatively gave the apostles the authority to make disciples as He had done and indicated that this system was to continue to the end of the age.

Matthew 10:19, 20 — Jesus indicated that the apostles were to be empowered by the Holy Spirit so that the Spirit of God would speak through them.

John 16:13 (and context) — Jesus told the apostles that they would be guided into all truth.

Luke 24:48, 49; Acts 1:8, 2:1–4 — Jesus promised to send the Holy Spirit upon the apostles, and the Holy Spirit would empower them to be His witnesses. This was fulfilled

1

in Acts 2:1–4. Subsequently in the book of Acts, when the apostles speak, they speak as they are led by the Holy Spirit.

Matthew 16:19, 18:18 — What the apostles "bound on earth" would be bound in heaven—in the sense that it would have already been bound; thus, their proclamation of the gospel was given according to a heavenly pattern.

Ephesians 2:20 — Because the Lord revealed His will through the apostles and prophets, they were part of the foundation of the church.

1 Corinthians 7:40 — The apostles were aware that they had the Spirit of God.

1 Thessalonians 2:13 — The word spoken (and written) by the apostles was the word of God.

1 Peter 1:22–25 — The good news that people obeyed to become Christians is spoken of as the living and abiding word of God.

1 Corinthians 2:12, 13 — The apostles had received the Spirit from God, and imparted what they taught in *words* taught by the Spirit—even the words were inspired.

Galatians 1:8, 9; Jude 3 — Because what the apostles taught was from God, it was considered authoritative. One who departed from it was guilty of apostasy and in danger of eternal condemnation.

Philemon 8, 9; 2 Thessalonians 3:6, 14, 15: 1 Corinthians 4:18–21 — The apostles made it clear in their letters that they had the right to require the church to do what they said (since they were inspired men who had a special role in the church—see 2 Cor 12:12).

Colossians 4:15, 16; Revelation 2:3 — What the apostles wrote to specific churches was, and was intended to be, circulated among other churches—this also witnesses to the authority of the apostles and the inspiration of their words.

2 Thessalonians 2:2; 3:17 — The apostles were concerned that the church accepted other (apparently fraudulent) writings as if those documents came from them.

Notes on the Canon of the New Testament

MEANING OF THE WORD

A. THE WORD "CANON" COMES ORIGINALLY FROM A word meaning "reed."

B. Apparently the "reed" was used to measure. Thus the word came to mean something like a "measure" or standard.

C. The word still has this significance in some contexts. One might, for instance, speak of the "canons of literary criticism," meaning the standards or rules by which literary criticism takes place.

D. With regard to the Bible, it came to mean those books which had met the standard, and thus it is applied to those books which are considered as inspired and therefore authoritative. In the New Testament, 27 books are said to be "canonical" and belong to the New Testament canon.

THE BOOKS WHICH BELONG TO THE CANON

A. Generally, the 66 books of our Bibles have been accepted for the past 17 or 18 centuries almost universally as canonical.

B. In addition to these books, Roman Catholics accept another group of books as part of the Old Testament and therefore as canonical. We call these books the *apocrypha*.

- Apocrypha is a word that means something like "hidden" and has the connotation of "spurious."
- Catholics sometimes speak of them as the "deuterocanon," the second canon, to distinguish them from the rest of the Old Testament books, which are thought of as the "protocanon," the first canon.
- It is interesting that some of the major and most important Greek manuscripts of the Bible include the apocrypha.

C. There are other books that have never been recognized as canonical which profess to relate to Old Testament characters or events. These books are known as the *pseudepigrapha*, a word that suggests the idea of false writings—or falsely attributed writings since many of them falsely claim to have been written by great men of the Bible.

D. There are also writings that relate to the New Testament in the same way. See *Handbook of Biblical Criticism* by Soulen.

THE SIGNIFICANCE OF THE QUESTION OF THE CANON

A. We should feel obliged to obey the will of the Lord as it is revealed in His word, the Bible. But we have no obligation to obey anything that is not found in books which are not inspired and therefore authoritative. It is important, therefore, that we feel assured that the books that we accept as canonical really belong in the Bible, God's word.

B. But questions are sometimes raised about the canon:

- The apocrypha may cause questions.
- Martin Luther questioned the value of the book of James. He never went so far as to exclude books from the New Testament canon, but relegated several books to the back of his Bible, indicating that they were not as valuable as others.
- Others today are raising questions. (See Carson, Moo, and Morris, *An Introduction to the New Testament*.)

THE ORIGIN OF THE CANON

A. What were the earliest attempts at coming up with a list of books that were to be regarded as inspired and authoritative, and when did they occur?

- Marcion's list (*CMM*, 492).
- Muratorian list (*CMM*, 492).

- Eusebius of Caesarea, indebted to Alexandrian fathers Clement and Origen (*CMM*, 492, 493).
- Athanasius's letter.
- Council of Carthage.
- Perhaps the most interesting thing is that there arose such universal agreement regarding the canon (*CMM*, 494).

B. Carson, Moo, and Morris say that three tests were applied to determine if books were canonical (*CMM*, 494, 495). Harrison speaks of the same criteria, using the following designations (Harrison 110, 111):

- Apostolic origin.
- Reception of the writings by the original churches and their continued knowledge of them.
- Consistency of doctrine, with the standard already possessed in the Old Testament and with the teachings of the apostles.

C. What shall we conclude from this?
   1. Should it concern us that we don't have earlier evidence of a "canon"—a list of inspired books?
   2. The most important questions are:

- Do we have the right books in the canon? There is near unanimity of opinion on the subject.
- Did the church give us the canon? No. Rather the books are inspired and authoritative;

therefore, they are accepted by the church and are in the canon.

THE PROCESS OF "CANONIZATION"

— A theory—

A. Jesus had all authority.

B. He authorized the apostles to speak with His authority. Churches had to heed their instructions.

C. What they spoke was regarded as inspired and authoritative. The word "tradition" was used for these teachings.

D. What they wrote was also regarded as inspired and authoritative.

E. As a corollary, what was written by those close to the apostles was regarded as inspired and authoritative.

F. What they wrote was circulated among the churches.

G. Eventually their writings began to be collected and circulated together.

H. When it became necessary to define what books were regarded as inspired and authoritative, the list consisted of those books that had long been circulating and had long been accepted as inspired and authoritative.

DOUBTS ABOUT THE CANON

A. If this is reasonable, why then did there continue to be questions about some of the books?

B. Usually it is possible to see some reasons why various individual books were not accepted as readily as others.

- Some of the general epistles
- Hebrews
- Revelation
- Books that were short, written to several churches, had "doctrinal problems," and were anonymous.

C. These doubts do not negate the positive evidence that the books were, for the most part, accepted early and widely among those who followed Christ. Add to that the fact that no apocryphal writing came close to receiving the same amount of support as the canonical books.

The Textual Criticism of the New Testament

WHAT IS "TEXTUAL CRITICISM"?

A. It has been defined as the "art and science of recovering the original text of a document." (Holmes, "Textual Criticism," chap. 4 in *New Testament Criticism and Interpretation*, ed. Black and Dockery, p. 101). Or, at least, recovering the best text possible.

B. It has also been called "lower criticism," to distinguish it from "higher criticism," which is concerned, e.g., with the "sources" from which the original text of a book was produced.

WHY IS TEXTUAL CRITICISM NECESSARY?

A. Our English Bibles are translations of the Greek New Testament. The New Testament books were originally written in Greek.

B. The Greek New Testament has been put together

from ancient Greek manuscripts. "No autograph of any classical, biblical, or early patristic writer is extant today." (Holmes, 101)

C. Originally, and for centuries (until the 15th century), copies of the scripture were made by hand.

D. This made it inevitable that mistakes in copying would be made. Once made, at least some of those mistakes would be passed on from one copy to another.

E. That such mistakes were made and passed on is evident from the differences in the ancient manuscripts which are available to us. There are many such differences— called variants—in the manuscripts.

F. From this array of imperfect manuscripts with all their variants, the textual critic attempts to reconstruct the text as the Biblical writer first penned it.

G. The work of textual critics is evident in:

- The text of our English Bibles. Compare the KJV with later versions: Mark 16:9–20; John 8:1–11; Acts 8:37; 1 John 5:7, 8.
- Footnotes or references in reference Bibles or study Bibles. See, e.g., Romans 16:25–27; Ephesians 1:1; 1 Peter 5:3.

HOW HAS TEXTUAL CRITICISM DEVELOPED?

A. During the Middle Ages, there was little interest in the original language of the New Testament. The language of the church and therefore of scripture was Latin.

B. At the dawn of the Reformation there was a renewed interest in the original languages of the Bible.

C. Erasmus published the first printed Greek New Testament in 1516. This went through various revisions but became the basis of what became known as the *Textus Receptus* (first called that in 1633)—the *Received Text*.

D. This Greek text remained the basis for the further translations of the New Testament, even though additional manuscript discoveries were made and work was done on the text, through the 19th century, when various scholars attempted to produce an improved text.

E. The most important improved Greek text was produced by Westcott and Hort in 1881. They identified four genealogical groups of manuscripts: Syrian (latest), Western, Alexandrian, and Neutral (usually preferred by Westcott and Hort).

Other theories have followed.

- One is that there is another text type known as the Caesarean, discovered by Streeter. See page 24 of House, *Chronological and Background Charts of the New Testament*.
- Today, according to Holmes (106, 107), three broad text types are recognized: Alexandrian, Western, and Byzantine (the least valued).

G. At the present time there is disagreement about how the textual critic should work.

- Some, in effect, reject all the work that has been done and argue for the received text.
- Some are in favor of the Majority Text—in every case where there are variants, the reading

favored by the majority of the manuscripts should determine which variant is to be chosen.

- Some favor "Thoroughgoing Eclecticism," or "Rigorous Eclecticism," "which relies virtually exclusively on internal considerations and places little if any weight on external evidence" and "treats the MSS as little more than a storehouse of readings to be evaluated on other grounds." (Holmes, 113)
- The majority of textual critics favor "Reasoned Eclecticism." See Holmes, 112.

H. The Greek text which is favored today is: Nestle-Aland, 28; and UBS 5.

HOW DOES THE TEXTUAL CRITIC WORK?

A. What are the sources available to the textual critic? With what evidence does he work? According to Harrison, the textual critic works with three sources:

1. Greek manuscripts

- Uncials—capital letters, generally earlier than the minuscules. Some of the leading manuscripts of the Greek New Testament are in this category: Vaticanus (B), Sinaiticus (Aleph), Alexandrinus (A), etc.
- Minuscules—small letters
- Lectionaries—collections of scriptures used in worship
- Papyri—the earliest.

2. Versions, or translations: Syriac (Diatessaron, Old Syriac, etc.), Latin, Coptic, etc.

3. Quotations from church fathers (patristic citations) in Greek or Latin.

B. What kind of evidence does the textual critic consider?

1. External (Holmes, 114).

2. Internal (Holmes, 115).

a. Transcriptional. Errors which are unintentional or intentional.

- Unintentional: caused by eyesight (misread, skip something, repeat something [Harrison, 85]), hearing, memory, and judgment.
- Intentional: spelling and grammar, harmonization, filling in or adding details, clarifying problems, conflation (combining manuscripts), doctrinal.

b. Intrinsic. "The aim is to evaluate readings in light of what an author is most likely to have written" (Holmes, 115).

C. On what basis does the textual critic decide? Three basic "rules" which guide the textual critic are (Harrison, 86):

1. The shorter reading is to be preferred over the longer.

2. The harder reading is to be preferred over the easier.

3. The reading is to be preferred which will most readily explain the origin of the other reading or readings.

SINCE THERE ARE MANY VARIANTS IN THE ANCIENT MANUSCRIPTS, SHOULD WE LOSE CONFIDENCE IN THE NEW TESTAMENT?

A. The variants are many—in the thousands!

B. Some may have let this fact cause them to lose confidence in the Bible.

C. But I would say "No," for the following reasons:

- Because of the number of ancient witnesses to the text of the New Testament. There are more witnesses to the text of the New Testament than to the text of any other ancient writing.
- Because of the general consistency of those witnesses. E.g., since the KJV was translated there have been hundreds of manuscript discoveries. But compare the KJV with the later versions to see, generally, how small the differences are.
- Because of the work of the textual critics. A great deal of work has gone into this effort. Although textual criticism is not and cannot be absolutely objective and "scientific," its practice tends to confirm our confidence in the overall accuracy of the New Testament Greek text.

- Because of the nature of the variants. The numbers don't tell the whole story. See Harrison's quote from Hort, 72.

APPENDIX

Types of Errors found in Manuscripts
Notes from a lecture given by Steve Williams1

I. Unintentional
    A. Eyesight
    1. Misread
    2. Skipped

- Haplography — skip a line, a word, or part of a word
- Palimpsests — text scraped off and written over
- Homoeoteleuton — skip from one line to another line that ends the same
- Dittography — repeat a word or phrase

    B. Hearing — via dictation
    1. Pronunciation
    C. Memory
    1. Synonyms substituted
    2. Sequence of words varied
    3. Letters in a word transposed
    4. Passage reworded as remembered in another gospel: (a) Why do you call me good? Ask: What's good? (b) Blessed are the poor; blessed are the poor in spirit.

D. Judgment

1. Copiest — unknowledgeable, sleepy, careless, in a hurry, etc.

2. Explanatory remark in margin incorporated as text — angel troubling water and jumping in to be healed. Not in early text.

II. Intentional Changes

A. Spelling and Grammar — especially in apocalypses

B. Harmonization — e.g., in gospels. Also, the Old Testament quoted in the New Testament—see Hebrews 12:20.

C. Additions — to fill in.

1. Matthew 9:13 — KJV — "to repentance" is added. In Gospels: Late MSS have "and Pharisees" after "scribes" more than early.

2. Galatians 6:17

- Early — the marks of Jesus
- Late — the marks of the Lord Jesus
- Later — the marks of the Lord Jesus Christ
- Latest — the marks of our Lord Jesus Christ

D. To Clarify Problems

1. Mark 1:2 — adds "Isaiah said." Changed to "in the prophets."

2. Matthew 27:9

3. Hebrews 9:4 — altar of incense in holy of holies; some early scribes changed it to holy place.

E. Conflation —combine manuscripts in order not to leave out a word.

1. Luke 24:53 — KJV — in temple praising and blessing God, conflated from:

- Early text — in temple praising God
- Another manuscript — in temple blessing God

F. Doctrinal.

1. Luke 2:41 and 43 says "his parents," referring to Joseph and Mary; later changed to Joseph and Mary.

2. Mark 9:29 — prayer and fasting. Fasting added by monks.

G. Miscellaneous Additions.

1. Revelation 4:8 — God is holy, holy, holy. Some 4, some 6, some 7, some 8, some 9, one 13.

2. Titles are miscellaneous additions.

3. Further down in the Byzantine — more additions. E.g., "the revelation of the all glorious evangelist, ..."

Endnotes

[1] Joel Stephen Williams, "Textual Criticism and Bible Translations," *Gospel Light* 63.12 (1993),184–85.

Suggestions Regarding Translations

1. KEEP THE ISSUE OF TRANSLATIONS IN PERSPECTIVE. Almost everyone agrees that anyone can be saved if he/she reads almost any translation (there are probably some exceptions—the *New World Translation* of Jehovah's Witnesses, for instance) *as a whole* and obey it. (Furthermore, most would not want to accept the logical consequences of asserting that any particular translation is necessary to salvation.) God did not call us to convert people to a translation or to dispute with brethren about translations, but to save the lost and to build up churches.

2. When you are doing personal work—teaching someone one-on-one in his/her home—it is always best, if possible, to allow the person you are studying with to use his/her own translation.

3. Every translation is imperfect. Few, if any, would argue that any translation is absolutely without fault. Thus, the issue really is: What version best expresses the original *in this particular verse?*

4. The ultimate test of a translation is whether or not it faithfully represents the original (or says to the reader in the new language what the reader in the original language heard), not whether or not it agrees with a favorite translation or a particular interpretation.

5. Most (probably 99 percent) of those who discuss translations are not qualified to judge for themselves the relative merits of differing Greek texts. (To do so would require them to examine and judge the relative merits of the manuscripts on which the different Greek texts are based. Even if one had the ability to do so, it is doubtful that he/she would have the opportunity or time to do so. It is also questionable whether to do so would be an efficient use of a minister's time.) Therefore, they will all always have to base their opinion on what others say about those texts. The question becomes: Whose word shall they take?

6. A translation should be evaluated on the basis of the purpose of its translator(s) and his (their) methods. To learn about such things, the student should read the forward or introduction to any translation he/she is thinking about using. For example: The *Amplified Bible* was never intended to be read in public. *Today's English Version* (*Good News for Modern Man*) is in simplified English for a purpose—and that's why it is so different. A paraphrase should be judged and used as a paraphrase, not as a literal translation. The difference between the New International Version and the New Revised Standard Version (and other translations that adhere to the tradition that extends from the King James through the American Standard to the Revised Standard) is largely a matter of a difference in translation theory and practice.

7. All else being equal, in translation there is "safety in numbers." Translations by committees are more likely to be trustworthy in their entirety than those by individuals. However, in particular verses, the best rendering may be from a translation by an individual (e.g., Phillips's).

8. A literal (word-for-word) translation is not always the best translation for two reasons: (1) It will probably be hard to read. (2) A word-for-word translation may not best express the meaning of the original language. However, there is value in a more literal translation since it leaves less room for interpretation on the part of the translators, and thus gives less opportunity for their biases to become part of the translation. But there may also be value in a freer translation in that it may better get across the original idea (though in different words).

9. Every translator has biases or preconceived notions, and the reader should watch for these to show up in the translation. However, the translator's biases will not necessarily be reflected in the translation. Conservatives often assume that liberal translators will offer corrupt translations. But this is not necessarily true, for two reasons: (1) Perhaps the highest value of scholarship is to be honest and deal fairly with the evidence; liberal scholars in general also embrace this value. (2) Liberal scholars (defining "liberal" as those who do not believe that the Bible is inspired, who do not believe that Jesus was raised from the dead, etc.) have no reason to offer a corrupt translation because they don't believe the Bible anyway (at least, not as we do). They have no problem saying, "This text reflects the idea that people believed that Jesus was raised from the dead, but in fact it didn't happen."

10. For study and exegesis, one should use a number of translations. In fact, it may be said that the best translation is a variety of translations. (However, one should also avoid the tendency to search through two dozen translations until he happens to find one that suits his predetermined understanding of what a word or verse means.)

11. It may be best for the preacher to choose one primary translation that he uses in preaching and teaching. If he does have a favorite translation that he uses most of the time or exclusively, he should also be aware of the translations that others use and know what those translations say in any passage he is discussing.

12. It is well for the preacher to encourage the use of a variety of translations within a class. This helps the students understand better how the Bible came into existence and also can help in the explanation of otherwise difficult passages.

13. It is not necessary nor wise to try to force people who have been using the King James Version all their lives to quit using it. However, if this version is used, the meaning of antiquated words and difficult passages must be explained thoroughly. Furthermore, the preacher needs to find a way to help people understand that what really matters is the original text of which the KJV is a translation.

14. In my opinion, it is unwise to ask children or people who have never read the Bible before to begin their study of scripture by using the King James Version. To do so places an unnecessary stumbling block in their way. They must learn to read a different language with strange words before they can begin to understand what the Lord would have them do

to be saved. There is no evidence that the Lord wanted the language of scripture to be hard to read.

Notes on the Gospels

INTRODUCTION TO THE GOSPELS AS A UNIT

A. The word "gospel" comes from the Greek word *euaggelion* which means "good news."

B. We usually think of the first four books of the New Testament as being four gospels. In one sense they are. But in another sense, there is only one gospel—one story of the life of Christ—and there are four accounts of that gospel.

- This idea is supported by the names of the gospels. They are called "the gospel according to ... ." In Greek: *kata Matthion*, e.g.
- These titles are not original, but it can be argued that they are very early—probably as early, in most cases, as the first century. It is reasonable to believe that at least as soon as there were two gospels written and known, it was necessary to identify each one by the name of its author.

C. What about the four books we know as gospels?

1. What are they?

- Matthew, Mark, and Luke are alike. Known as "synoptic gospels" or "synoptics." "Synoptic" means "seeing together."
- John is different. For differences between John and synoptics, see the chart "Contrasts Between the Synoptics and John" (House, 95).

2. Why four? No one knows.

- It was thought by some early church fathers to be inevitable and right that the church should have four gospels.
- This we can say: four witnesses to the life and teachings of Christ give us both better evidence for the reality of the events portrayed in the gospels and a greater appreciation for the Christ. Seeing Him from four angles is better than seeing Him from only one. We might compare the beginnings of the four: we would be poorer if we lacked any of them.

C. What is their genre? "Genre" is a French word for "kind, sort, style." Its equivalent in German is *Gattung*, which "denotes a group of things or beings which have important or distinguishing [i.e., 'typical'] characteristics in common" (Soulen, 75, 76). Thus, it is a particular kind of literature.

We call them "biography," but they are obviously different from today's typical biography:

- Little information about the childhood, youth, and early adulthood of Jesus. Mostly they tell about His public ministry, beginning from the time He was thirty.
- Very selective: they give details of only about 50 days out of the 12,000 days that Jesus lived.
- Relatively great amount of space spent on the last week of Jesus's life.

2. There is disagreement among scholars.

- Some say that they are a unique genre, that there is nothing else exactly like them in the literature of the first century.
- Most believe that they are somewhat like the biographies that were written in ancient times but with very significant differences.

D. The gospels and history.

1. Are the gospels history? Do the gospel writers intend to write history? Yes and no.

a. No, in that what they write is not mere history, only history, disinterested objective history. (But is there such a thing? I suspect that every historian has a purpose, a point to make, in writing history). What they write is, in a sense, theology—a religious message about what God did through Christ to bring salvation to mankind. They are, in a sense, sermons.

b. Yes, in that:

- What they write is historically accurate. Some
  doubt it, but there is good reason to believe in
  the historicity of the facts reported in the
  gospels.
- What they claim is that *God acted in history*:
  God sent His Son to earth in history, at a
  particular moment, to a particular place, and His
  Son assumed flesh and walked about on the
  earth, died an actual death in a literal place, and
  was raised from the dead, at which time He
  bodily (literally) came forth from the tomb. It is
  the historical aspect of Christianity that
  separates it from most of the other religions of
  the world.

2. If the gospels are history, how can their differences
from one another, their discrepancies, and their alleged
contradictions, be explained? Such discrepancies exist.

a. These discrepancies can be overemphasized. The
gospels, including both John and the synoptics, in several
respects tell the same story, the main points of which are (see
Harrison, 141, 142):

- Jesus's ministry was prepared for by the work of
  John the Baptist.
- In His public ministry, He both taught and
  performed miracles.
- At the end of His public ministry, He spent
  about a week in Jerusalem and at the end of that

time He was crucified, at the command of
Pontius Pilate and at the insistence of the Jews.
- He was raised from the dead.

b. There are ways to explain the differences.

(1) See, for example, DeHoff, *Alleged Bible Contradictions Explained*; McGarvey, *Evidences of Christianity*; Geisler and Brooks, *When Skeptics Ask*, 173–175.

(2) The main thing to remember is: Two statements are contradictory only if both *cannot* be true.

(3) Other important points to keep in mind:

- The gospel writers have different purposes; apparent contradictions may be the consequence of their different purposes.
- The gospel writers may use different organizing principles; one may be more chronological, another more topical.
- Jesus was capable of teaching a wide variety of subjects and emphasizing different things, depending on His audience and their needs.

c. Today the major emphasis is not so much to explain the differences as to emphasize the individual gospels.

- It seems reasonable to compare and harmonize the gospels. This has been done since the time of Tatian's *Diatessaron* in the late second century. To say the least, when we are teaching or preaching from one of the gospels, we need to know when differences exist and be able to say something about those differences.

- But it is true that the first readers of a particular gospel probably did not have all the other gospels in hand at the time they were reading one. They learned from that gospel the particular message it taught. Just as they studied the gospels, as it were, one at a time, it is also a good idea for us to study the gospels one at a time.

E. The purpose of the gospels. Why were the gospels written? Several possibilities exist.

1. To preserve in permanent form the teachings of the apostles and evangelists about Jesus. They contain a deposit of the teachings of those who were closest to Jesus, regarding His life and teachings. It was to be expected that their teachings would be committed to writing.

2. To provide a guide for the church. The disciples of Christ needed a record of the life and teachings of Christ so that they might know what to believe and how to behave and so that they might have greater assurance of the truth that they had accepted.

a. Some teach that what Jesus taught is not directly applicable to Christians today—especially what He taught about marriage, divorce, and remarriage—since Jesus lived and died under the Law of Moses.

b. There are at least two objections to this point of view:

- It seems strange to say that Christ's disciples should *not* listen to their Master's teachings, either then or now.

- While Christ lived and died under the Law of
  Moses, the gospels were obviously written after
  —some long after—the establishment of the
  church for the benefit of those who lived during
  the Christian age.

3. Perhaps to help refute false doctrine, from false
teachers both within and outside the church. Certainly, the
gospels would have served this purpose, even if the gospel
writers were not writing with this in mind.

4. To help in the evangelization of the lost. This seems
especially obvious in the purpose statement for John's gospel:
John 20:30, 31.

THE SYNOPTIC PROBLEM

A. What is the synoptic problem?

1. The fact that three of the gospels are alike, and one
(John) is different.

2. But more than that: it is the extent of the similarities
that creates a problem. See, e.g., tables 2 and 3 in *CMM*, 26,
27. See also the table on page 143 of Harrison. These are not
just similarities in ideas, but the use of the same words to
recount the same story. Allen Black (*An Outline of New
Testament Introduction*, 1994, 27) notes that there is a high
degree of similarity in:

- the choice of material.
- the order of the pericopes.
- the wording of events.

B. Why is this a problem?

1. It's not necessarily a problem that should shake our faith. The synoptic parallels and John's dissimilarity do not disprove inspiration. Furthermore, one can fruitfully study and preach from the gospels without "solving" the problem (as it is defined below). But it is a problem in that (if we are to study the gospels from a carefully informed and scholarly standpoint) it needs to be explained. The fact is that in the Bible God does not usually inspire different writers to say *exactly* the same thing. What explanations are there? (See Harrison, 144–150.)

- The synoptic accounts are all original. The gospel writers came up with the same words on their own or by inspiration without any knowledge of one another's works.
- The synoptics all get their words from the same oral tradition.
- The synoptics all use a common source which is not the same as any one of the synoptics.
- The synoptics use one another in some way. One is the source of another. This is the alternative usually preferred by New Testament scholars.

C. How have scholars tried to solve this problem? Three methods of critical study (from *CMM*, 20–45; see these pages for an evaluation of each of the following):

1. Form Criticism: Focuses on the preliterary form of the tradition. Attempts to discover the original *Sitz em Leben* (setting in life) of the stories and sayings that make up the gospel accounts. Tries to accomplish this by analyzing the

forms in which those stories and sayings are found. It is thought that by discovering the forms, one can say something authoritative about how those forms were used in the early church, and so one can know the setting in life of a particular saying or story.

2. Source Criticism: Seeks to discover the written sources that lie behind the gospels. Opinions vary as to how many sources there were and how they were used.

3. Redaction Criticism: Attempts to analyze how the writer, who was primarily an editor or redactor, used the sources at his disposal. By comparing the synoptics, one can know how the redactor used his sources: what he left out, what he included, what he expanded, and what he changed. By studying this, one can know the redactor's major concerns, emphases, and purposes.

D. What about the sources of the gospels?

1. What sources have been suggested? There are four source theories for the synoptic gospels:

a. The Augustinian hypothesis: Matthew's gospel was first; Mark used Matthew; and then Luke used Matthew and Mark.

b. The Griesbach hypothesis: Matthew's gospel was first; Luke used Matthew; and then Mark used both Matthew and Luke. This view has been revived in recent times by Farmer and others.

c. The two-source theory: Mark and Q. Q stands, apparently, for German *Quelle*, or source. It is used for the material which is common to Matthew and Luke but which is not found in Mark.

- Q is usually thought to have been a written source. But some who use the expression do not necessarily think of a written source, but only of the material common to Matthew and Luke which is not found in Mark.
- By either definition, Q consists largely of the teachings of Jesus.
- The two-source theory, which accepts the priority of Mark, is most commonly held today, whereas until this century it was usually believed that Matthew was the first gospel written.

d. The four-source theory: Mark and Q and M (for material peculiar to Matthew) and L (for material peculiar to Luke). For a diagrammatic presentation of these views, see pages 88, 89 of House.

2. Can one believe that the gospel writers used sources and still believe that they were inspired? Yes, because:

- Old Testament writers apparently used sources. See the books of history.
- Apparently, Luke used sources or did research (Luke 1:1–4).
- If early Christian writers are to be believed, Peter was Mark's source.
- The general rule in inspiration is that God inspired people who already know something about what they are going to write (for example, who are eyewitnesses) and then guides them in the writing so that the results are exactly what

He wants. If He can guide a writer in the use of the information the writer already has, He can also guide a writer in the acquisition of information through research and the use of sources.

3. We do not have to subscribe to any particular theory regarding the synoptic problem to be able to appreciate and understand each of the synoptic gospels. All we have to do is simply to read and study each one on its own terms and we will be able to get from it what God intended.

Notes on Matthew

INTRODUCTION

I. MATTHEW IS THE FIRST GOSPEL IN THE NEW Testament.

II. Until the nineteenth century it was generally assumed that Matthew was the first gospel written. (*CMM*, 32.) It was believed that the other gospel writers used Matthew as a source. (Harrison, 142.) "This gospel, according to the citations found in early Christian writers, was used more than any of the other gospels." (Guthrie, 28.)

III. This changed in the nineteenth and twentieth centuries with the view that Mark was the original gospel and that Matthew and Luke used Mark as a source. Mark became the gospel most studied, and Matthew was relatively neglected.

IV. Nevertheless, Matthew remains of great value.

AUTHORSHIP

A. Matthew and the synoptic problem.
  1. Matthew, Mark, and Luke are the synoptic gospels.
  2. The most commonly accepted theory today is:

- Mark has priority.
- Matthew and Luke both used Mark as a source.
- In addition, both Matthew and Luke used another (hypothetical) source, named "Q," probably for the German *Quelle*, "source," consisting primarily of the teachings of Jesus.
- This accounts for the material which Matthew, Mark, and Luke have in common, and which Matthew and Luke have in common but which is not found in Mark.
- In addition to these two sources, it is sometimes theorized that Matthew used another source for the material which is peculiar to Matthew alone, a source sometimes known as "M."

  3. All of this is speculation, of course. It fails to take into account that Matthew was an apostle and had first-hand information about much that he wrote; he was an eyewitness.
  4. On the other hand, there is nothing inherently wrong with believing that Matthew used sources. An inspired writer can use sources; God inspires him in the way he uses those sources. The close similarity between the words used by the synoptic writers argues for a literary relationship between the three gospels.

B. Did Matthew write the gospel of Matthew?

1. Evidence in favor:

a. The title: "According to Matthew."

b. Papias's statement, via Eusebius: "Matthew composed the sayings in the Hebrew (or Aramaic) language, and each interpreted (or translated) them as best he could." (*CMM*, 68)

(1) This is evidence in favor of Matthew's authorship of the gospel, but it is difficult because:

(a) It is hard to know how to translate the statement in Eusebius.

(b) There was a tradition that Matthew first wrote his gospel in Aramaic (or Hebrew). (See Guthrie, 46–48.) But there is no surviving copy of the gospel of Matthew in Aramaic. And there is some evidence that Matthew wasn't first written in Aramaic and later translated into Greek.

- Matthew doesn't sound like "translation Greek."
- Most of Matthew's quotations from the Old Testament are from the Septuagint (LXX).
- Matthew apparently makes use of Mark, which was written in Greek.

(c) As a result:

- Some (*CMM*, e.g.) suggest the possibility that Papias was right about Matthew's authorship but wrong about the language in which he first wrote.

- Some believe that perhaps Papias or others confused the gospel of Matthew with another gospel originally written in Hebrew.
- It may be possible to translate or interpret the passage by Papias in such a way as to remove the difficulty it presents.
- Some have thought that Matthew wrote a gospel in Aramaic, which was used by Mark, and then wrote the gospel in Greek, using Mark.

c. Other evidence has been cited—e.g., Matthew alone refers to himself as a tax collector (Matt 9:9; 10:3).

2. Evidence against, alternative theories:

- One argument: "Matthew, an apostle, would not have used Mark, who was not an apostle, as a source." But Mark, according to tradition, wrote down Peter's gospel.
- An alternative theory: Matthew was the product of a community or a "school," not of an individual author.

C. What do we know about this Matthew? Relatively little:

1. He was an apostle (Matt 10:2–4; Mark 3:16–19; Luke 6:12–15; Acts 1:13). The apostles were chosen to be eyewitnesses of the resurrection (Acts 1:22; 2:32), and "to be with [Christ] and to be sent out to proclaim the message" (Mark 3:14).

2. He was a tax collector (a publican) (Matt 9:9; 10:3).

Tax collectors had a bad reputation (see, e.g., Luke 15:1) but were not necessarily bad people.

3. It is possible that he was quite prosperous (Matt 9:1off; Mark 2:15ff).

4. He was also named Levi (Mark 2:13–15).

DATE

A. If Matthew used Mark, it had to have been written after Mark. There is good reason to believe that Mark wrote down the gospel that Peter preached. One early church father has Mark writing before Peter's death; another, after his death. If Mark is the source of Luke, then it could be argued that Mark wrote before or about AD 60. In such a case, Matthew had to have been written after AD 60.

B. Matthew is quoted by Ignatius of Antioch soon after AD 100, so it could not have been written after that.

C. Many scholars favor a date after AD 80 or 85. This would not be impossible.

D. But it seems more likely that Matthew would have been written before the destruction of the Temple in AD 70. (See *CMM*, 78, 79.) So it might be best to guess at a date in the middle-60s.

PLACE OF ORIGIN

A. Because of Matthew's "Jewishness," it has been thought that the book originated in Palestine.

B. The other possibility suggested is Antioch of Syria, primarily because that is where it was first quoted or cited (by Ignatius).

DESTINATION, ADDRESSEES

A. It is usually assumed that the author wrote for the benefit of those among whom he worked.

B. Since the book seems to have been written with the Jews in mind, it is probable that it was written for Jewish Christians and/or for Christians (whether Jewish or Gentile) who lived among a large Jewish population.

CANONICITY

"The gospel of Matthew was universally received as soon as it was published and continued to be the most frequently cited gospel for centuries" (*CMM*, 81).

OUTLINE, STRUCTURE

The following are from Black, 35:

A. Geographical/Life of Jesus. This is the oldest division scheme:

- Birth
- Preparation for ministry
- Galilean ministry
- To Jerusalem
- In Jerusalem.

B. Five discourses, each ending with the formula "and when Jesus had finished these sayings ..." First proposed by B. W. Bacon, 1918. Based on five speech blocks: 5–7, 10, 13, 18, 24–25.

Outline:

- 1–4 Prologue
- 5–9
- 10–12
- 13–17
- 18–23
- 24–27
- 28 Epilogue

C. Kingsbury's three sections, based on the formula "from that time … " (which is also found in 26:16):

- 1:1–4:16   Person of Jesus
- 4:17–16:20   Proclamation of Jesus
- 6:21–28:20   Passion of Jesus

CONTENTS, CHARACTERISTICS, EMPHASES

A. Matthew follows the typical chronological sequence of the synoptics: ministry of John the Baptist, ministry in Galilee, triumphal entrance into Jerusalem, final week, death, and resurrection. In addition, along with Luke, it provides information about the birth and early life of Jesus.

B. It emphasizes the teachings of Jesus. It has been thought to be primarily a gospel organized around Jesus's teachings; see above.

C. It gives some evidence of being arranged topically. It is very systematic. See Black, 35.

D. There seems to be an emphasis on the kingdom.

Notice that the wise men come seeking him who is born king of the Jews (Matt 2:2).

E. Matthew is the one gospel that uses the word "church" (Matt 16:18).

F. It is thought to have been written for the Jews.

1. In various ways it speaks to a Jewish audience.

- It begins with the genealogy of Jesus. But it traces that genealogy back to David and to Abraham, two of the greatest figures in Israel's history, and also two from whom the promised Messiah was to come. Contrast this with the starting point of Luke's genealogy—Adam.
- It speaks of the kingdom as "the kingdom of heaven," whereas other gospels use the expression "Kingdom of God." This suggests a Jewish interest, since the Jews, seeking to avoid saying the name of God, would tend to substitute "heaven" for "God" if they could.
- There is also a great emphasis on the fulfillment of Scripture in the book, particularly by the use of the expression "... that it might be fulfilled."
- There is also the command: Go not to the Gentiles . . . (Matt 10:5, 6; 15:24).

2. But more needs to be said about this characteristic of the book. Although Matthew has these Jewish characteristics:

a. It is not particularly complimentary to the Jews.

- Here we find the very strong words of Matthew 23.
- We also find the threat, promise, or prediction, that the Jews as a nation would be cast out. See: Matthew 21:31, 32; Matthew 21:41–45 (cf. Mark 11:9 and Luke 20:16); Matthew 8:10–12.

b. And Gentiles are pictured in a good light as coming to Jesus: the wise men, the centurion (Matt 8), a Canaanite woman (Matt 15:21–28), the Great Commission.

3. What does the evidence suggest concerning the gospel's relationship to the Jews? Matthew seems to have both a polemic purpose (to be an attack) and an apologetic purpose (to be a defense): to argue against Judaism and for Christianity, and to demonstrate the "rightness" of Christianity's spread beyond the Jews to the Gentiles. Specifically, it does the following:

a. It demonstrates that there is plenty of evidence to prove that Jesus is the Christ, the Messiah for whom the Jews have been looking.

b. It answers their questions. If they ask, "What about God's promises to the Jews?", then Matthew's answer is: Christ gave the Jews every opportunity to accept the truth (He came first to them), and by their rejection, they sealed their own doom. Their guilt is obvious, and their condition as rejectors is graphically displayed in the gospel.

c. It explains that by their rejection, they opened the door to the Gentiles, who are now fitting subjects for the kingdom of heaven.

PURPOSE(S)

A. Two preliminary points need to be kept in mind (see also *CMM*, 80.):

1. The writers of the synoptic gospels obviously shared some of the same purposes. Their similarities should not be overlooked. They were all written to present an account of the historical Jesus and His teachings.

2. It would be impossible to isolate a single purpose for any one gospel.

B. For Matthew, in addition to those purposes which Matthew had in common with the other synoptics:

1. To teach the church. Matthew 5:20 — a call to better righteousness. (Black, 35)

2. To present the relationship between Christ, on the one hand, and Judaism and the law, on the other hand. (See also *CMM*, 81.)

Notes on Mark

AUTHOR

A. MARK'S AUTHORSHIP HAS BEEN ATTESTED BY VARIOUS patristic writers:

1. By Justin, who cites Mark's gospel and says the citation is found in "Peter's memoirs." (Black, 31); Clement of Alexandria; Tertullian; Origen; and Jerome, who identifies Mark as "John Mark." (Black, 31,32)

2. Also by Papias (quoted in Eusebius), writing in the first third of the second century and quoting "John the elder" (perhaps John the apostle), who says that Mark wrote the gospel, that he "was not an eyewitness but obtained his information from Peter, and that his gospel lacks 'order'" (*CMM*, 92).

B. Mark's place among the synoptic gospels:

1. The synoptic gospels are Matthew, Mark, and Luke. The word suggests the idea of "seeing together." They are

gospels that present the gospel of Jesus in the same way. They are remarkable in that they contain, not only the same message but, to a great extent, the same words.

2. The most common view today is that Mark was written first. What are the arguments for Mark's priority? *CMM*, 32–34, lists the following:

- The brevity of Mark.
- The verbal agreements among the Gospels. "Careful study reveals that, while all three accounts sometimes agree ... . Matthew and Mark frequently agree, as do Mark and Luke, but Matthew and Luke only rarely agree." (p. 33)
- The order of events. "Matthew and Luke do not agree against Mark." (p. 34)
- Mark's awkward and more primitive style.
- Mark's more primitive theology. "This argument has some weight but is not as decisive as the ones above." (p. 34)

C. What the New Testament says about Mark:

- Acts 12:12 — His mother was Mary, in whose home the church met to pray after Peter was imprisoned. Family of means?
- Acts 13:4 — Assisted Barnabas and Paul on the first missionary journey.
- Acts 13:13 — Turned back at Perga in Pamphylia.
- Acts 15:36–39 — Point of contention between Paul and Barnabas when they got ready to go on

the second missionary journey. Went with Barnabas to Cyprus.

- Colossians 4:10 — With Paul when Paul was in prison, the cousin of Barnabas. See also Philemon 24.
- 2 Timothy 4:11 — Paul asked for Mark to be sent to him, as Paul neared the end of his life, saying that Mark was useful to him.
- 1 Peter 5:13 —He is with Peter, who calls him his son, in Babylon, which is generally thought to be a code name for Rome.
- There is a possibility that the young man referred to in Mark 14:51, 52 is Mark.

D. According to tradition, he writes Peter's gospel. See *CMM*, 106, for a comparison of Peter's message in Acts 10 with an outline of Mark's gospel.

E. Probably the title of Mark, *Kata Markon*, "according to Mark," was added very early, when other gospels were known, and may even be original. Notice: there is only one gospel! Each of the four is *the gospel* according to ... a different author.

DATE

A. Dates from the 40s through the 70s have been suggested. There is little evidence to favor the 40s, and generally, the 70s have been suggested because the book supposedly pictures the destruction of Jerusalem (ch. 13) after the event —an unwarranted conclusion if one believes that Jesus could foretell the future.

B. Data and conclusion

1. If Mark was used as a source by Matthew and Luke, it had to be written earlier than they.

2. If Luke/Acts was written at the end of the two years Paul spent in Rome, it had to be written about 62. Thus Mark had to be written earlier.

3. If Mark was written from Rome for Romans, especially if Peter was in Rome at the time, then it (probably) had to be written after Romans (since there is no indication that Peter was in Rome or had been in Rome when the book of Romans was written). Romans was probably written from Corinth at the end of the third missionary journey (Acts 20:3), about 56.

4. This would mean that Mark wrote before Peter died, contrary to some traditions.

5. But if these assumptions are accepted, Mark could have been written anytime between, say, 57 and 60, and could have still been used by Luke.

6. The best alternative to this date is the middle 60s, before or after Peter's death and at about the time of Nero's persecution.

PROVENANCE

There is evidence to indicate that Mark was written from Rome. (See *CMM*, 95, 96). Notice especially 1 Peter 5:13 and compare Mark 15:21 with Romans 16:13.

TEXT

The major issue regarding the text has to do with whether Mark 16:9–20 was a part of the original text of Mark.

A. The evidence is somewhat ambiguous, but thought by the authors of the text to favor leaving it out.

B. One major question that should be raised is: If Mark 16:9–20 was not part of his original work, why would Mark end his gospel in the way he did? Verse 8 is hardly a satisfactory ending for a gospel. The explanations which have been offered are not very satisfactory.

C. It should be remembered that no essential of the Christian religion is affected even if Mark 16:9–20 is rejected.

CHARACTERISTICS, AUDIENCE, AND PURPOSE

A. Characteristics

1. Mark is the gospel of action, of movement. It omits any mention of Jesus's pre-existence, birth, or childhood, and gets immediately into the story of His life, and particularly of His miracles. Notice the use of "immediately" (Gk. *euthus*) in the gospel: e.g., 11 times in Mark 1 alone (10, 12, 18, 20, 21, 23, 28, 29, 30, 42, 43).

2. Mark emphasizes Jesus's miracle-working power. It pays comparatively less attention to the teachings of Jesus. But it frequently gives more space to the narratives of Jesus. E.g., the paragraph about the feeding of 5,000 in the *Harper Study Bible* (RSV): Matthew — 9 verses, 17 lines; Luke — 8 verses, 18 lines; Mark — 15 verses, 25 lines. (John — 14 verses, 23 lines)

3. Mark is the gospel of vivid detail. Mark 6:39 — "on the green grass."

4. Mark places great emphasis on the death of Christ. *HSB*: "The events of the last week in Jerusalem occupy over one-third of the book with the climactic end of the ministry dominating the entire account." According to one man, Mark is "a passion narrative with an extended introduction" (*CMM*, 101).

B. Audience

1. It seems obvious that Mark was written for Gentiles. See Mark 7:3, 4 and 15:22, 34.

2. Perhaps more specifically, a Roman audience.

- Many "Latinisms." Mark 12:42 — coinage is explained in Roman terms. (Black, 32.)
- There is also the tradition that it was written in Rome.
- Furthermore, the characteristics of Mark would make it a gospel especially suitable for a Roman audience. The Romans would be interested in the powerful Son of God who could perform miracles. Compare Mark 1:2 and 15:39.

C. Purpose

1. Mark probably had more than one purpose in mind: perhaps to record the history of Jesus for posterity, and to provide help in evangelism.

2. In addition to this, the following deserves consideration.

a. In the first (approximately) half of the book, Mark

places great emphasis on the power of Jesus as evident in His miracles. He is therefore the powerful Son of God with all authority.

b. In the second half of the book, Mark places equally great emphasis on Jesus's suffering and on the fact that His disciples are also called to suffer, to deny themselves, to become servants. See Mark 8:34–38; 9:35–37; 10:35–45.

c. So perhaps Mark's purpose was not only to present Christ as the powerful Son of God, for the benefit of his particular audience but also to make clear what true discipleship meant.

STRUCTURE

Black (p. 33) suggests the two following outlines for the book:
   A. Geographically

* Galilee 1–6:13
* Mostly outside of Galilee   6:14–8:26
* To Jerusalem   8:27–10:52
* In Jerusalem   11:1–end

B. Structure centered on the major themes of Christology and Discipleship with a focus on 8:27–30—the Christological turning point.

1. Before 8:27–30, disciples don't know who Jesus was.

2. After 8:27–30, Jesus explains His future death. And the disciples are taught to take up their cross.

Conclusion

A major achievement: If Mark was indeed the first gospel, then he, by inspiration, produced a new kind of literature—biography, but more than biography—a gospel (See *CMM*).

Notes on Luke

INTRODUCTION

I. LUKE IS THE THIRD OF THE SYNOPTIC GOSPELS. THE most common view is that Luke (along with Matthew) used Mark as a source, as well as using (also with Matthew) another source, known as "Q."

II. Luke was a prolific writer. His two-volume work, Luke/Acts, comprises just over 25% of the New Testament. Luke is the longest gospel.

RELATIONSHIP TO ACTS

A. It is obvious that Luke and Acts were written by the same person.

1. They are addressed to the same person. See Luke 1:1–4 and Acts 1:1, 2.

2. They exactly dovetail or fit together. Compare the end of Luke with the beginning of Acts.

3. They are similar in vocabulary and style. Davis's *Dictionary of the Bible*: the "vocabulary and style of the two books are notably alike." Similarly, Carson, Moo, and Morris write, "The style and vocabulary are what we would expect from the same author ..." (113).

B. Thus, the two books are counted as one—usually referred to as Luke/Acts—and the gospel of Luke is seen as the first volume of a two-volume work.

AUTHOR

If Luke and Acts were written by the same person, who is this person? Tradition has assigned authorship to Luke, Paul's companion.

A. In favor of Luke as the author of Luke/Acts:

1. Early writers assigned the book to Luke: Marcion, the anti-Marcionite prologue, the Muratorian Canon, Irenaeus, Tertullian, and "the oldest MS of Luke, Bodmer Papyrus XIV, cited as P^{75} and dated to AD 175–225" (*CMM*, 113).

2. Biblical evidence favors Luke. The author can be determined from the "we" sections in Acts.

a. Acts 16:10 — with Paul and Silas at Troas, 2nd journey.

b. Acts 16:11–16 — travels with Paul to Philippi, is with him there, but not with him when he goes on to Thessalonica (Acts 17:1). (Stays in Philippi?)

c. Acts 20:5–8 — at the end of 3rd journey, joins Paul at Philippi as Paul travels back to Jerusalem.

d. Acts 20:13–15; 21:1–18 — accompanies Paul to Jerusalem. (Paul goes to Caesarea bound as a prisoner [Acts

23:31–33]; there is no mention of the author, but probably he makes the same trip on his own.)

e. Acts 27:1–28:16 — accompanies Paul on his trip from Caesarea to Rome.

f. Thus, the author was with Paul in Rome.

- Who were those who were with Paul in Rome, according to the prison epistles? Colossians 1:1 — Timothy. Colossians 4:10–14 — Aristarchus, Mark, Jesus Justus, Epaphras, Luke, and Demas. Ephesians 6:21 — Tychicus. Philemon 1 — Timothy. Philemon 23 — Epaphras, Mark, Aristarchus, Demas, Luke. Philippians 1:1 — Timothy. Philippians 2:25 — Epaphroditus.

- "Of these, Epaphras and Epaphroditus did not arrive in the company of Paul, hence could not have described the sea voyage [and the epistles specify how they did arrive]. Tychicus, Aristarchus, Timothy, and Mark are ruled out because they are all mentioned at some point in the Book of Acts in the third person. Demas later deserted the apostle, making the identification dubious. Further, there is no tradition in his favor as author. Two remain, Jesus called Justus and Luke. Since there is no indication that the former was with Paul during the events reported in the 'we' sections, and since patristic testimony to his authorship is lacking, Luke only is left, and he is supported by the tradition ..." (Harrison, 196, 197; see also *CMM*, 113, 114).

g. So the author of Luke and Acts is Luke.

3. Another argument that has been made in the past is that Luke/Acts contains an abundance of medical terms which would point to Luke, the "beloved physician," as the author. Even though the language is consistent with a medical background, this is not now regarded as strong proof of Luke's authorship (*CMM*, 114).

B. Objections to this point of view.

1. *CMM* say that only the theological objections have any merit (188, 189)—and they don't have much:

- Paul's use of Stoic philosophers in Acts 17 is inconsistent with Paul's teaching in Romans 1.
- The Paul of Acts is loyal to the law, but the Paul of the letters teaches that Christians are not under the law.
- The Paul of Acts lacks the emphasis on union with Christ and the expiatory benefits of Christ's death that is so central in the Paul of the letters.
- The preaching of the Paul of Acts is uneschatological (too interested in church government, e.g.).

2. None of these objections is convincing.

C. What do we know about Luke?

1. He was a companion of Paul. See above.

2. He was called the "beloved physician" (Col 4:14).

3. He was probably a Gentile. Notice that after naming three men who are with him Paul says "these are the only men of the circumcision among my fellow workers for the kingdom of God," but then he goes on to mention three other

men, including Luke. (Col 4:7–14) Apparently, these three men were Gentiles. This would be in keeping with some of Luke's emphases; see, e.g., the genealogy of Jesus he includes. See also Acts 1:19.

4. He was likely well-educated. His gospel is the most literary of the gospels and uses a preface that is typical of literary works of the day. He writes in "good Hellenistic Greek" (*CMM*, 115).

PERSON(S) ADDRESSED

A. The person addressed.

1. Theophilus. The name means "lover of God."

2. "Most excellent" is used elsewhere by those who are government officials. (See Acts 23:26; 24:3; 26:25.) This may suggest that Theophilus was some kind of government official.

3. It has been suggested that this is a way of saying: To all who love God. But most think this is unlikely, and that it is far more likely that Theophilus was an actual person.

4. He may have been Luke's patron, paying the cost of publication (*CMM*, 117).

5. Luke probably had a larger audience than just one person in mind; other works dedicated to one person were really written for a larger audience. Compare Josephus's work *Against Apion*, a two-volume work dedicated to Epaphroditus (Harrison, 202).

B. The larger audience.

1. It has been usually thought that Luke was written for Gentiles, particularly for Greeks.

a. The emphasis on Gentiles—all are descended from

Adam, the gospel is preached in all the world—would suggest a Gentile audience.

b. "Ramsay notes that Luke's care to inform his readers about points on the geography of Palestine, even the simplest, is in sharp contrast to his assumption of geographical knowledge on their part for the Greco-Roman world" (Harrison, 202).

c. Luke also avoids the use of Semitic expressions, such as "rabbi" and "Hosanna" (Harrison, 202).

d. The Greek preface and the good quality of the language also might suggest a Gentile audience.

2. Others think it might have been a Jewish Christian audience. According to Jervell in *Luke and the People of God*, Jewish Christians were under fire from non-Christian Jews, especially for embracing Gentiles (Black, 37).

DATE AND PROVENANCE

A. Date

1. The best guess is about 62, after Paul had spent two years in a Roman prison (Acts 28:30, 31), but before his trial and before the results of that trial were known. Otherwise, it is hard (but not impossible) to imagine any good reason why the results of the trial would not have been included.

2. If Luke used Mark, then Luke was written after the gospel of Mark.

3. But Paul's use in 1 Timothy 5:18 of Luke 10:7 suggests that Luke was written before 1 and 2 Timothy, and before Paul's death, thus before about 65.

4. Many scholars date Luke/Acts later, but their reasons for doing so are not convincing.

B. Provenance: Place of origin.

1. It could have been written from Rome, while Paul was at Rome, for Romans.

2. An early tradition claims that Luke was a native of Antioch of Syria and that the place of writing was Achaia.

PURPOSE

The purpose of Luke needs to be considered along with the purpose of Acts.

A. What Luke said: See Luke 1:1–4.

1. "Many" had written about the events before Luke wrote.

2. Luke distinguishes himself from those who were eyewitnesses.

3. He investigated everything carefully "from the very first." (NRSV)

4. His aim: "to write an orderly account ..." Thus, to write an accurate two-volume work on the beginnings of Christianity.

5. So that Theophilus (and other readers) might "know the truth concerning the things about which you have been instructed." (NRSV)

B. Other possibilities:

1. CMM discusses and dismisses proposed purposes for Acts (thus for Luke/Acts) focused on conciliation, evangelism/apologetics, and theological polemics, and then concludes in favor of a theological and pastoral purpose, saying that Luke has a number of purposes in his two books which all "are part of a larger, general purpose--the edification of Christians" (198).

2. To use in Paul's defense at his trial in Rome.

3. As a missionary document. Luke sets the stage for the mission work of the church. Acts continues and completes the story, describing how the gospel indeed went into all the world, by going to Rome, the center of the world.

4. To reassure the faith of the readers. After listing seven possible purposes discussed in an article by Maddox, and indicating that the seventh—to reassure the faith of the readers—is the most valid, Black endorses the following purpose for Luke/Acts which he says is a modification of Jervell's ideas:

> Luke wrote a reliable account of the story of God's fulfill-
> ment of his prophetic promises of salvation to reassure
> Christians that their story was truly the fulfillment of
> God's plan despite the rejection of this explanation by the
> Jewish leadership and the acceptance of many uncircum-
> cised Gentiles and such fringe groups as Samaritans, tax
> collectors, and eunuchs (Black, 38).

CONTENT

A. Black provides the following "geographical/life of Jesus" outline: Prologue, infancy, preparation for ministry, Galilee, travel narrative, and Jerusalem events (Black, 37).

B. "The infancy stories (1–2) and the travel narrative (9:51–19:27) are Luke's most distinctive sections" (Black, 37). For other lists of material exclusive to Luke (*CMM*, 127; House, 92).

CHARACTERISTICS

A. Luke is a historian.

1. He alone among the gospel writers sets Jesus' story in history (Luke 2:1, 2 and 3:1). Generally he has been shown to be a reliable historian.

2. Questions have been raised because other evidence seems to indicate that the census by Quirinius was taken in AD 6, obviously too late for this to be the time for the birth of Christ. But there are various suggestions which satisfactorily explain this apparent discrepancy. See Harrison, 203, 204; Walter L. Liefeld, "Luke," in *Expositor's Bible Commentary*, 8:843.

B. Luke is a "literary" author. "Renan called this gospel the most beautiful book in the world" (*CMM*, 127). Regarding his style:

1. He writes good Greek.

2. The infancy narrative, Luke 1, 2, is very much in the style of the Septuagint.

C. Other characteristics

1. *CMM* (127–132): gospel of salvation; universalism; interest in those "who were generally held of no account in the first century: women, children, the poor, and the disreputable;" the Holy Spirit; prayer; song and joy.

2. Black (38): fulfillment of prophecy, restoring of Israel and saving of Gentiles, saving of outcasts of Jewish society, divine reversal—low lifted up and high brought down (see Luke 1:51–53), material possessions and almsgiving, prayer, Holy Spirit.

Notes on John

INTRODUCTION

THE EARLIEST KNOWN WRITING OF THE NEW Testament is a fragment of John, dating from about AD 130 (Carson, Moo, and Morris, 172). See also Harrison, 216.

AUTHOR

Much of the following information comes from Bruce, *The New Testament Documents: Are They Reliable?*

A. The title of the book provides evidence that it was written by John.

B. Internal Evidence

1. The book speaks of "the disciple whom Jesus loved." See John 21:24; 13:23; 19:26; 20:2ff. The gospel claims that this is the person who wrote the gospel. Who was it?

- Had to be one of the apostles, because they were the only ones present when Jesus announced that one would betray Him (Mark 14:17).
- It seems most likely that it would have been Peter, James, or John (Mark 14:33).
- It was not Peter, because Peter is named in the fourth gospel (John 13:24; 20:2; 21:20).
- It was not likely to have been James, because of his early death (Acts 12:2).
- It is interesting that John the apostle is not mentioned by name in this gospel.
- And that "John the Baptist" is just called "John." Why? Perhaps because it was not necessary to distinguish him from John the apostle, since John the apostle was the author of the gospel.

2. John the apostle would be a suitable author from the standpoint of the characteristics of the book:

- It claims to be written by an eyewitness (John 21:24) and the book bears evidence of this. John was an eyewitness.
- It also appears to have been written by a Palestinian. John was a Palestinian.
- And by a Jew. John was a Jew.

C. External Evidence

1. Ignatius, who died about 115, was influenced by the distinctive teaching of the gospel.

2. Polycarp quotes from the first epistle.

3. Justin Martyr, about 150, quotes from the story of Nicodemus in John 3.

4. Tatian, about 170, included the gospel in the *Diatessaron*, and in fact made it the framework into which he blended the material from the other gospels (*CMM*, 140, 141).

5. Irenaeus testifies that John wrote a gospel.

6. The Muratorian fragment says John wrote the gospel.

7. The Anti-Marcionite prologue testifies that John wrote the gospel.

8. "Certainly from the end of the second century on, there is virtual agreement in the church as to the authority, canonicity, and authorship of the gospel of John" (*CMM*, 141).

D. Objections to the idea that the apostle John is the author. Arguments against John's authorship are based on the nature, style, and wording of the book itself (*CMM*, 146–151). Among those arguments are:

1. John, a native of Galilee, could never have written a book that deals so much with Judea.

2. John, being "unschooled and ordinary" (Acts 4:13), could not have composed a gospel in good Greek, or one of such "subtlety and depth." But, see *CMM* (147): "There is now a powerful consensus that at least in Galilee, and perhaps elsewhere in first-century Palestine, the populace was at least bilingual, and in some cases trilingual."

3. John, a "son of thunder" (Mark 3:17), could not have composed so loving and placid a book.

4. John wanted to call down fire from heaven upon the

Samaritans (Luke 9:54); he could never have written a book that dealt so kindly with the Samaritans (John 4).

5. John the apostle would not have called himself "the disciple whom Jesus loved."

E. Alternatives to the authorship of John the apostle.

1. Some believe that there was another John, rather than the apostle John, who wrote the gospel, basing their understanding on a quotation from Papias found in Eusebius. See *CMM*, 142, 143.

2. Some believe that the gospel was produced by a "Johannine Community." According to this theory, the gospel in its various parts would have been produced over a period of time in reaction to problems faced by the community.

F. Assuming that the author was John the apostle, what do we know about him?

1. Son of Zebedee and brother of James (Matt 4:21).

2. They were fishermen, owned a boat, and had hired servants (Mark 1:19, 20).

3. May have been a disciple of John the Baptist (John 1:35–40).

4. James and John were partners of Peter in the fishing business (Luke 5:9, 10).

5. Called by Jesus to be a "fisher of men" (Matt 4:21; Mark 1:19, 20).

6. Appointed to be an apostle (Matt 10:2).

7. With James, called "Sons of Thunder" by Jesus (Mark 3:17).

8. Rebuked one who cast out demons in Christ's name but was not of their company (Luke 9:49).

9. Wanted to call down fire on a Samaritan village that did not accept Jesus (Luke 9:52–54).

10. With James, sought a place of special honor in the kingdom (Matt 20:20–24; Mark 10:35–41).

11. One of three disciples Jesus chose to be with Him on special occasions:

- Raising of Jairus's daughter (Mark 5:37; Luke. 8:51).
- Transfiguration (Matt 17:1; Mark 9:2; Luke 9:28).
- Gethsemane (Matt 26:37; Mark 14:33).

12. Sat next to Jesus at the Last Supper (John 13:23). Was called the "disciple whom Jesus loved."

13. Probably the one who followed Jesus and entered the court of the high priest, who was known to the high priest (John 18:15, 16)

14. Accepted responsibility for Jesus's mother (John 19:27).

15. Ran with Peter to investigate the report of the empty tomb (John 20:1–10).

16. Undoubtedly as an apostle he saw the risen Lord.

17. Jesus spoke of him while talking to Peter (John 21:20–23).

18. Waited in Jerusalem after the resurrection, along with the other apostles, for the Holy Spirit. (He is listed second.) (Acts 1:13).

19. Involved in a healing and subsequent imprisonment (Acts 4,5).

20. Along with Peter, sent from Jerusalem to Samaria after the first converts were made there (Acts 8:14ff).

21. With the other apostles remained in Jerusalem when the disciples scattered (Acts 8:4). Still there, as one of the "pillars" of the church, when Paul visited Jerusalem (Gal 2:9).

22. Credited with writing five books of the New Testament: John, 1 John, 2 John, 3 John, and Revelation.

23. Tradition says that he served his later ministry for many years in Ephesus.

24. When he wrote the book of Revelation, he was on the island of Patmos, presumably an exile, because of the testimony of Jesus (Rev 1:9).

25. Tradition also says that he was the last apostle to die, and the only one to die a natural death.

PROVENANCE AND DATE

A. Place of writing. Four possible places have been suggested: Alexandria, Antioch, Jerusalem, and Ephesus. Because of patristic testimony, Ephesus is usually thought to be the place of writing.

B. Date. Dates from before 70 to the final quarter of the second century have been put forward (*CMM*, 166).

- A very late date is ruled out by manuscript discoveries. (See above.)
- But a later date is generally accepted, in part because of the words of John 21:20–23. *CMM* argues for 80–85.

PURPOSE

The book itself states its purpose. See John 20:30, 31.

A. The verse emphasizes major themes of the gospel.

1. "Jesus did many other signs ...which are not written . ..
But these are written ..." *Signs* are emphasized. Seven miracles, called signs, performed by Jesus, are found in the book
(not including the resurrection).

- John 2:1ff — water into wine
- John 4:46ff — healing of an official's son
- John 5:1ff — healing of a man paralyzed for 38 years
- John 6:1ff — feeding 5,000
- John 6:15ff — walking on water
- John 9:1ff — healing of man born blind
- John 11:1ff — raising Lazarus from the dead

2. "... so that you may come to believe..." *Belief* is emphasized. "The verb 'believe' is used 100 times in the book"
(Black, 43).

3. "...that Jesus is the Messiah [the Christ], the Son of God ..." *Jesus as the Son of God* is emphasized. In part through the "I am " sayings:

a. "Before Abraham was, I am" (John 8:58). This is obviously a claim to divinity. Especially so since God said to call Him "I am" (in Greek, *ego eimi* in both the Septuagint and the New Testament).

b. "I am" followed by a metaphor:

- The bread of life (John 6:48)

- The light of the world (John 8:12)
- The door of the sheepfold (John 10:7)
- The good shepherd (John 10:11)
- The resurrection and the life (John 11:25)
- The way, the truth, and the life (John. 14:6)
- The true vine (John 15:1)

4. "...and that through believing you may have life in his name." *Life* is emphasized.

B. The idea of the verse may be that the book was written to help Christians continue to believe or to help non-Christians come to believe. If the latter, then the book itself says it has an evangelistic purpose.

C. Other possibilities: Polemic against Gnosticism, polemic against a John the Baptist group, polemic against Jewish attacks (emphasizing the evil Jewish leaders) (Black, 43).

STRUCTURE (from Black, 43)

- 1:1–18   Prologue
- 1:19–12   Public Ministry (book of signs)
- 13–20   Passion and Resurrection (book of glory)
- 21   Epilogue

CHARACTERISTICS (from Harrison, 212–215)

A. The style is simple.

B. The thought is profound.

C. Outstanding elements of language:

- non-theological terms that relate to style,
- terms that bear more definitely on the message but are used almost as frequently in one or more of the Synoptic Gospels,
- terms bearing on the message of the book whose use so far exceeds that in the other Gospels as to be outstanding—e.g., words for witness, believe, live and life, love (verb and noun), abide or remain, truth and true, Jew, world, feast, and possibly light.

D. A prologue and epilogue, miracles called signs, discourses that reveal the person of Christ and feature the "I Am" sayings.

E. Emphasis on the national feasts or festivals of the Jews and Jesus's attendance upon them.

F. Considerable part of the activity of Jesus in Judea rather than Galilee.

G. Jesus is not often pictured as addressing great throngs of people, but more often pictured as talking with individuals.

H. The deity of the Son is given great prominence.

I. Pivotal to the understanding of this Gospel is the place Jesus occupies in relation to Judaism, fulfilling its legitimate hopes and opposing its aberrations.

J. Purpose with regard to Synoptics: Not to supplant, perhaps to supplement, but especially to delineate the person and work of Jesus in such a way as to interpret their deeper significance.

PROBLEMS

A. Text: The most important textual variant is the story of the woman taken in adultery—John 7:35–8:11. *CMM* cites evidence which they feel justifies the conclusion that the story was not a part of the original text (particularly not where it is found in John) (*CMM*, 172, 173).

B. Relationship with Synoptics

1. Greatly different from the Synoptics. See House, 95. See also Black, 44, which points out that John differs in many areas:

- geography,
- chronology,
- omissions,
- reserve (or lack of it) with which Jesus speaks of His Messianic claims.

2. How can those differences be explained, and reconciled?

a. Black suggests four ways to "bridge the gap between John and the Synoptics":

- Harmonize.
- Emphasize Jesus's versatility as a teacher.
- Emphasize different audiences for Jesus's teachings.
- Defend the legitimacy of John's paraphrasing of Jesus's speech in a looser way than do the Synoptics.

b. We also need to remember that John was, probably,

- written at a different, later, time;
- to a different audience with different needs;
- for a different purpose;
- with knowledge of the Synoptics or of their contents in mind (i.e., John's gospel is deliberately different).

Notes on Acts

INTRODUCTION

I. ACTS IS THE ONE BOOK OF HISTORY IN THE NEW Testament. Carson, Moo, and Morris (195) reject other possibilities and say that it belongs to the "category of ancient history."

II. Acts is significant. It bridges the gap between the gospels and the epistles. It tells us how the church began. It gives us a picture of the church and how people got into the church. It also tells what Jesus continued to do and how He did it.

III. But it may not be a very popular book to many.

NAME

A. It belongs with Luke, as the second volume of a two-volume work on Christian beginnings.

B. It has been called by various names. See *CMM*, 181.

We know it as Acts of Apostles. But not all of the acts of all of the apostles are included in it.

C. *CMM* (181): "Judging from Luke's own emphases, he may have preferred a title such as 'The Acts of the Holy Spirit' or 'What Jesus Continued to Do and to Teach'" (see 1:1).

AUTHOR

Luke. See "Notes on Luke."

TO WHOM WRITTEN

A. Theophilus. Means "lover of God." "Most excellent" is used elsewhere by those who are government officials. Probably a specific individual.

B. But the book Luke-Acts was probably written for a larger audience than just that one individual. See "Notes on Luke."

DATE

A. The best guess is about 62 after Paul had spent two years in a Roman prison (Acts 28:30, 31), but before his trial and before the results of that trial were known. If Paul had been tried and the outcome of the trial was known, why not include it (especially since the book has been moving towards Paul's Roman imprisonment since Acts 21:27)?

B. There are possible answers to that question:

1. Another volume might have been intended and planned, but never completed.

2. If the purpose is to help Paul at his trial, then obviously it would not be necessary to go beyond the imprisonment in Rome.

3. If the primary aim of the two-volume work relates to mission work, when Paul arrives in Rome, the center of the world, the story has been completed.

C. Nevertheless, it seems more reasonable to believe that it was written about 62.

PURPOSE(S)

(See "Notes on Luke.") The purpose of Luke needs to be considered along with the purpose of Acts.

A. What Luke said: See Luke 1:1–4. To write an accurate two-volume work on the beginnings of Christianity so that the readers might know the truth concerning it.

B. Other possibilities

1. Acts has a number of purposes which all "are part of a larger, general purpose—the edification of Christians." (*CMM*, 198)

2. To use in Paul's defense at his trial in Rome.

3. As a missionary document. Luke sets the stage for the mission work of the church. Acts continues and completes the story, describing how the gospel indeed went into all the world, by going to Rome, the center of the world.

4. In connection with this latter purpose, it could also be used to demonstrate how people were saved and added to the church. If we are to judge the purpose of a book by what that book contains and emphasizes, then we must be ready to explain the emphasis Acts puts on conversion.

5. There is also a major emphasis on how the gospel

overcame barriers until all were and could be a part of the kingdom of God.

CHARACTERISTICS

A. Luke is a historian. And has generally been shown to be a reliable historian.

B. Luke is also a "literary" author.

C. Acts is a missionary book.

D. Acts emphasizes the Holy Spirit.

E. Harrison, 241, 242:

- Distinctly a missionary document.
- Necessarily fragmentary. Doesn't tell everything.
- Emphasis on two centers, Jerusalem and Antioch, and two apostles, Peter and Paul.
- Speeches are prominent in Acts.
- Terms for speaking, preaching, and bearing witness are common.
- The Holy Spirit is the key to the success of the Christian mission.

OUTLINE

A. A two-part outline: Peter and Paul.

- Acts 1–12 is largely about Peter.
- Acts 13–28 is almost altogether about Paul.

B. A four-part outline (or three-part outline): Acts 1:8.

- Jerusalem — Acts 1:1–8:1
- Judea and Samaria — Acts 8:1–12:25
- "To the ends of the earth" — Acts 13:1–28:31

C. Black gives the following alternative outline based on Acts 1:8 (39), based on the understanding that this is not just a geographic outline of the book but also involves religio-ethnic categories:

- Prologue — (1:1–11)
- Jerusalem (Jewish) Mission — (1:12–8:3)
- Samaritan Mission — (8:4–25)
- Gentile Mission — (8:26ff)

D. A six-part outline, based on six summary statements found in Acts; for the following outline see Carson, Moo, and Morris, 181–185. Compare the outline in House, 123.

- Prologue: Foundations for the church and its mission (1:1–2:4).
- The church in Jerusalem (2:42–6:7).
- Wider horizons for the church: Stephen, Samaria, and Saul (6:8–9:31).
- Peter and the first Gentile convert (9:32–12:24).
- Paul turns to the Gentiles (12:25–16:5).
- Further penetration into the Gentile world (16:6–12:20).
- On to Rome (12:21–28:31).

CRITICAL ISSUES

A. The text of Acts: The Western Text of Acts is about ten percent longer than other manuscript families. However, this creates few problems, if any, for most of the additions are "harmless." See *CMM*, 201. For most readings, the Western Text is not followed.

B. The historicity of Acts: There has been, and remains, a great deal of skepticism about whether Luke accurately reported history in the book of Acts.

1. There are some problems—e.g., "Josephus seems to conflict with Luke 2:1, 2 over the date of Quirinius's governorship" (Black, 39), and Acts and Galatians seem to conflict over how many trips Paul made to Jerusalem.

2. Nevertheless, these differences can be reconciled, and in other ways, Acts has been demonstrated to be accurate. Sir William Ramsay began his study of the background of Acts as a skeptic but was convinced by his own research of the book's historicity.

C. The speeches in Acts. They make up 30% of the text. Are they an accurate representation of what was said? It is unlikely that they are word-for-word reports of all that was said—almost certainly the sermons and speeches were longer than 3–5 minutes! (Black, 39) Very likely they are, for the most part, summaries. But that does *not* mean that they are inaccurate.

D. The inconsistency in Paul's theology. It is claimed that Luke's representation of Paul's theology in Acts conflicts with Paul's theology as presented in his letters. See Black, 40:

- Paul's Attitude Toward Law
- Paul's Use of Natural Theology in Acts 17
- Paul's Christology in Acts
- Eschatology in Acts

E. The theology of Acts

1. According to Black (40), Acts has been criticized for advocating early catholicism, which involves such things as the following: a positive attitude toward the law, the historicizing of Jesus, the institutionalism of elders and sacraments, a theology of glory and not a theology of the cross, and offering guarantees of faith.

2. Obviously this is caused by coming to Acts with a preconceived notion of what Acts ought to teach and then criticizing it because it doesn't teach that.

Notes on the Epistles

INTRODUCTION

A. How many epistles are there? 21

B. Which books are the epistles? Romans through Jude

C. What percentage of the New Testament do they comprise? 35% of the New Testament text (Carson, Moo, and Morris, 231)

D. How are they divided? Basically into two categories:

- Pauline epistles — 13. Romans through Philemon
- General epistles — 7. James; 1 and 2 Peter; 1, 2, and 3 John, Jude.
- Hebrews has sometimes been classified as one of Paul's epistles—but it does not seem likely that Paul wrote Hebrews—and sometimes as one of the general epistles. It doesn't seem to fit well into either category.

DEFINING "EPISTLE"

An epistle is a letter. Are they like our letters?

A. Before we discuss that, we might ought to note that the epistles of the New Testament vary widely. There's a great deal of difference, for example, between Romans and Philemon.

B. But to answer the question: Are they like our letters (like the letters we usually write)?

1. They are like our letters in that

- they usually say to whom they were written and by whom and
- they generally include personal information about both the sender and the recipient.

2. But they are not like most of our letters in that

- they were, apparently, intended to be circulated and were circulated widely,
- they dealt with profoundly important topics and had extremely serious purposes, and
- for the most part, they give the impression of being written with great care and give evidence of good organization.

3. The difference between, on one hand, our letters (and most ancient letters) and, on the other hand, most of the letters of the New Testament, has led some scholars to differentiate between epistles and letters.

a. We might describe the difference as follows: An

epistle is a consciously literary work; a letter is very personal and makes no pretensions of being a work of art. If such a distinction is valid, then Philemon probably comes closest to being a letter and Romans might be thought of as an epistle.

b. *CMM* (233) note that Deissmann distinguished between epistles and letters, claiming that an epistle was a "carefully composed, public piece of literature," whereas a letter was an "unstudied, private communication." To him, all of the New Testament epistles were really letters. This distinction is not generally accepted by scholars today.

NEW TESTAMENT EPISTLES AND THE LETTERS OF THE ANCIENT WORLD

The New Testament letters share many characteristics with the letters of the ancient world.

A. Those letters were often dictated to an amanuensis (a secretary or scribe). So apparently were some (perhaps most) of Paul's letters. See Romans 16:22.

B. Those letters, after being written by a secretary, might be signed by the individual who had dictated the letter. Apparently, Paul used this practice also. See 2 Thessalonians 4:17; see also 2 Thessalonians 2:2; Galatians 6:11.

C. They were carried by an individual to the recipient.

D. Those letters generally followed a certain form—a form adapted and used by Paul (from Black, 6, 7):

1. Opening, including:

- Name of sender
- Name(s) of recipient(s)

- Greetings (in Greek world—*charein*, "greetings," in Paul—*charis*, "grace")

2. Prayer (sometimes found in ancient letters), usually for the health of the recipient. Paul generally includes such a prayer, for the spiritual health of his readers.

3. Body

4. Closing "farewell" and often date; often before "farewell" are greetings and a health wish. Paul does not use "farewell" and dates but closes with greetings and prayers or wishes. "May the God of peace be with you" is a common ending for Paul.

E. One way in which New Testament letters differed from others of their day is that they are generally longer than the samples of ancient letters that have been recovered. See *CMM*, 232.

OTHER CHARACTERISTICS OF NEW TESTAMENT LETTERS

A. Paul often associated others with him in the opening of the letter. Probably he did not intend for these to be thought of as co-authors. 1 Corinthians 1:1; 2 Corinthians 1:1; Philippians 1:1; Colossians 1:1; 1 Thessalonians 1:1; 2 Thessalonians 1:1; Philemon 1:1.

B. The letters were carried by hand from the writer to the recipients. See, e.g., Philippians 2:25, 29; Ephesians 6:21, 22; Colossians 4:7–9.

THE NATURE OF THE EPISTLES

The major point made with regard to epistles today is that they are "occasional" documents.

A. What does this mean? It means that each one was written to provide help with regard to a specific occasion, to solve a particular problem, or to speak to a particular need.

B. What does this mean for interpretation?

1. It is well for us to remember it since one of the most important rules of interpretation is that a passage should be understood in its own context. Thus, to understand any passage in an epistle, we need to try to understand the "occasion," the problem, and the situation, that caused the epistle to be written.

2. Allen Black also makes the point that "Paul's letters were occasional and ministerial" and that in them we find "not systematic but situational theology." (7)

3. However, we should not suppose that because the epistles were "occasional" documents we can learn nothing from them that establishes a binding pattern today. Since the epistles were written to correct wrongdoing and to encourage righteousness among churches and individual Christians, they presuppose the existence of a standard by which churches and Christians can be judged, and they bear witness as to what that standard included, and thus to what it includes today. The letters, therefore, occasional as they are, can be used to establish what Christ would have His people today do and be.

Notes on Paul's Life and Letters

THE IMPORTANCE OF PAUL

A. It would be hard to overemphasize the importance of Paul.

    1. He was the first great missionary, the founder of many churches, an instrument God used to spread the gospel throughout the Roman Empire ...

    2. the prototype for the gospel preacher ...

    3. the main character in the book of Acts ...

    4. the author of thirteen (some say fourteen) of the books of the New Testament ... (Paul is just behind Luke in the percentage of the New Testament written by one individual (Carson, Moo, and Morris, 215) ...

    5. and the premier theologian of the early church.

    B. Still we must reject the views that Paul is the real founder of Christianity and that Paul's view of Christianity was diametrically opposed to that of Peter.

PAUL'S LIFE

A. Major events and facts about his life.

1. He was also called Saul (Acts 8:1, 3; 9:1ff; 11:25; 13:2; 13:9; 13:13; 13:16). This may have been his Jewish name, whereas Paul was his Greek name.

2. He was a Jew, a member of the Pharisees (Acts 22:3; 26:5; Phil 3:4–6).

3. He was born at Tarsus in Cilicia (Acts 22:3; 21:39). Apparently educated (perhaps when he was older) with a Greek education. (See Acts 17:28; Titus 1:12,13; Acts 26:24.)

4. He was brought up in Jerusalem at the feet of Gamaliel, "according to the strict law" of the Jews (Acts 22:3).

5. He was a Roman citizen (Acts 22:25–29; 16:37–39; 23:27; 25:10–12).

6. He was a tentmaker (Acts 18:2, 3; Acts 20:34, 35).

7. He was possibly from a family that was on the upper end of the socio/economic scale. As a relatively young man, he had advanced far in his religion (Gal 1:13, 14; Phil 3:4–6). He may have been a member of the Sanhedrin council when Stephen was killed (Acts 8:1; Acts 26:10). The very fact that he was entrusted with the mission to Damascus illustrates the high regard with which he was held (Acts 9:1, 2). His nephew had access to Jews who had made a plot to kill him and also to the tribune (Acts 23:16–24).

8. He was, as a zealous Jew and Pharisee, a persecutor of Christians (Acts 8:3; 9:1, 2; 22:4, 5; 26:9–11; 1 Cor 15:9; Gal 1:13; Phil 3:6; 1 Tim 1:12–16).

9. Jesus appeared to him on the road to Damascus (Acts

9:4–6; 9:27; 22:6–8; 1 Cor 9:1; Gal 1:11, 12). This revelation of Christ called him to preach the gospel, especially to the Gentiles (Acts 26:16–18), and qualified him to be an apostle (1 Cor 9:1; Gal 1:1).

10. From that point he began to preach Christ in Damascus (Acts 9:19–25).

11. From Damascus he went away into Arabia and then returned to Damascus (Gal 1:17).

12. He next preached in Jerusalem (Acts 9:26–29).

13. He then went to Tarsus (Acts 9:30), where he stayed (perhaps as long as a decade—see *CMM*, 226) until Barnabas sought him to assist him in his work at Antioch of Syria (Acts 11:19ff; see esp. 11:25, 26). From Antioch Paul and Barnabas went up to Jerusalem with a gift for the brethren in Judea (Acts 11:27–30).

14. Working at Antioch with several others, Paul and Barnabas were called to take the gospel to the Gentile world (Acts 13:1, 2)—in keeping with his original call to be sent to the Gentiles (Acts 26:17, 18).

15. Paul and Barnabas went on the "first missionary journey" to Cyprus and Asia Minor and back. John Mark, Barnabas's cousin, accompanied them but soon turned back. They returned to Antioch (Acts 13, 14).

16. While Paul and Barnabas were in Antioch, the "Jerusalem conference" was held. They traveled Jerusalem to participate in it (Acts 15).

17. After the "conference," Paul and Barnabas agreed that they should go and revisit those churches established on the first journey, but could not agree on whether to take John Mark. Barnabas took Mark and went to Cyprus; Paul took Silas and went overland to visit the churches in Asia Minor

which had been established on the first journey (Acts 15:36–41). This begins the "second missionary journey" (Acts 15:40–18:22).

18. On the second journey, Paul crossed the sea into Europe and preached in Greece. From there he sailed to Syria, landing at Caesarea, and from there, according to the RSV, "went up and greeted the church [probably the church at Jerusalem], and then went down to Antioch" (Acts 18:22) before leaving again on the "third missionary journey" (Acts 18:23–21:15).

19. On the third journey, Paul traveled overland again to Ephesus (Acts 19), where he spent most of his time. His journey back took him through Macedonia (Acts 20:1) and Greece (probably Corinth, Acts 20:2), through Macedonia again (Acts 20:3), from which he sailed to Troas (Acts 20:6). He returned then to Jerusalem by ship, with a stop at Miletus to talk with the Ephesian elders (Acts 20:17). Without going to Antioch, after landing at Tyre he went to Jerusalem (Acts 21:7–15).

20. Apparently soon after he arrived in Jerusalem, he was arrested in the temple on a false charge (Acts 21:28). For the rest of the book of Acts, he is in custody, first in Jerusalem (Acts 21–23), then in Caesarea (Acts 23:31ff) for more than two years (Acts 24:26). As a Roman citizen, he appealed to Caesar (Acts 25:11), and so was eventually sent to Rome.

21. Paul's fourth journey in Acts is the journey to Rome (Acts 27, 28). After a shipwreck and after spending three months on Malta, Paul finally arrived in Rome, where he lived under guard in his own hired house with the freedom to teach whoever came to him (Acts 28:16–31).

22. There is evidence that Paul was acquitted at his first trial:

- The events in the pastoral epistles do not fit into an outline of his life; thus, he must have been released to have done those things that these epistles speak of.
- The prison epistles, in contrast to 2 Timothy, seem to suggest that Paul believed he would be released.
- There are traditions that Paul was released, that he did go to Spain, as he intended (Rom 15:24), and that Paul was martyred under Nero (which would require a later date for his death).

23. Probably Paul was acquitted at his first trial, released, did further missionary work, and was then martyred during the Neronian persecution.

B. Chronology

1. There is evidence outside the Bible that Gallia (Acts 18:12) "was proconsul of Achaia from July 51 to July 52" (*CMM*, 229) when Paul was in Corinth. This helps provide an *absolute chronology* of Paul's career, as contrasted with the *relative chronology* derived from considering his letters and the book of Acts alone. One can from the date for Gallia count back from that date to get close to the date of Paul's conversion, and forward from that date to date most of Paul's letters.

2. One problem in establishing a date for Paul's conversion is knowing whether the fourteen years of Galatians 2:1

should be added to the three years of Galatians 1:18, or whether it is to be regarded as a part of the fourteen.

3. The Carson, Moo, and Morris chronology (p. 231) (cf. House, 127–132):

- Conversion   A.D. 34–35 (or earlier)
- Ministry in Damascus and Arabia   35–37
- First Jerusalem Visit   37
- Ministry in Tarsus and Cilicia   37–45
- Famine-Relief Visit   45, 46, or 47
- First Missionary Journey   46–47 or 47–48
- Apostolic Council   48 or 49
- Second Missionary Journey   48 or 49–51
- Third Missionary Journey   52–57
- Caesarean Imprisonment   57–59
- Voyage to Rome   59–60
- Roman Imprisonment   60–62
- Ministry in the East   62–64
- Death   64–65

PAUL'S LETTERS

A. Paul wrote thirteen letters (not counting Hebrews). (His authorship of six of these is disputed by more liberal scholars; from those whose Pauline authorship is doubted most to those which are doubted least, they are: the Pastoral epistles, Ephesians, Colossians, 2 Thessalonians.)

B. They have been classified by Hiebert (*An Introduction to the Pauline Epistles*) as follows:

- Eschatological: 1 and 2 Thessalonians

- Soteriological: Romans, 1 and 2 Corinthians, Galatians
- Christological (Prison Epistles): Ephesians, Philippians, Colossians, Philemon
- Ecclesiological (Pastoral Epistles): 1 and 2 Timothy, Titus

C.   Possible Dates (from House):

- Galatians — late 48 or early 49
- 1 and 2 Thessalonians— 50 or 51
- 1 and 2 Corinthians — 54 and 55
- Romans — 55
- Philemon — 60
- Colossians — 60
- Ephesians — 60
- Philippians — 61
- 1 Timothy — 62
- Titus — 62
- 2 Timothy — 63 or 64

Notes on Romans

ADDRESSEES

A. THE CITY OF ROME:

- Capital of the Roman Empire, center of political importance.
- Large; a population of perhaps 4,000,000.
- Half free, but most of these poor; few rich; other half slaves.
- A large population of Jews, although Jews had earlier been driven out of Rome (Acts 18:2).

B. The church in Rome.

1. Was probably not begun by Peter. Why? Because Paul said he wanted to share with them "some spiritual gift to strengthen them" (Rom 1:11). If Paul here speaks of a miraculous gift of the Holy Spirit and if such a gift could only be imparted by an apostle (Acts 8:15–18), it would appear that

no apostle, including Peter, had been to Rome at the time that Paul wrote. Nor was it begun by Paul, because Paul had never been there (Rom. 1:13). See Carson, Moo, and Morris, 242.

2. Perhaps it had its beginning with some who had been converted in Jerusalem on the Day of Pentecost or later, who then returned to Rome (Acts 2:10).

3. Were the Christians in the church in Rome Jews or Gentiles? They were likely both since what Paul said has relevance to both, with perhaps a majority of Gentiles.

4. The church in Rome was justly famous, then and later (1:8). The letter contains no rebukes, though it does deal (in chapters 14 and 15) with a problem that apparently bothered the church in Rome.

5. Apparently the church in Rome met in homes (16:5).

C. Paul's relationship to the church in Rome.

1. Paul had not yet been to Rome. (1:9, 10; 15:22), but was planning to visit the church there (15:22–24).

2. But he had many friends there. See chapter 16. How could he have many friends in a church which he had never visited? It is possible.

AUTHOR

A. Paul. This is undisputed. Even those who doubt that Paul wrote many of the epistles ascribed to him believe that Paul wrote Romans.

B. Tertius was the amanuensis (Rom 16:22).

OCCASION AND DATE OF WRITING

A. What Paul had done and planned to do: Romans 15:18–24.

B. What Paul was doing:

1. was going to Jerusalem with aid for the saints (Rom 15:25).

2. was taking with him the money he had already collected from Macedonia and Achaia (Corinth) (Rom 15:26, 27).

3. When he had finished with that, he would go on to Spain and come by on his way to see them (Rom 15:28, 29.)

C. Thus, Romans was written after 1 Corinthians, which tells the church in Corinth to collect money for this need (1 Cor 16:1ff), and after 2 Corinthians which urges the church in Corinth to do what they had planned to do (2 Cor 8, 9).

D. It was also written after Paul had visited Macedonia to collect their offering.

E. 1 Corinthians was written while Paul was in Ephesus on the third missionary journey—"But I will stay in Ephesus until Pentecost" (1 Cor 16:8; see Acts 19:21)—and 2 Corinthians was apparently written from Macedonia as Paul started the trip back to Jerusalem (2 Cor 7:5–15; Acts 20:1).

F. Thus, Romans was written in Corinth during the three months Paul spent there as he continued his journey towards Jerusalem at the end of the third missionary journey (Acts 20:2, 3). The date would have been about 56 or 57. That he was in Achaia or Corinth, is confirmed by:

- Phoebe was from Cenchrea, Corinth's seaport to the east (16:1).

- the presence of Gaius; (16:23) cf. 1 Cor 1:14
- the presence of Erastus; (16:23) cf. 2 Tim 4:20 ("Erastus remained in Corinth")
- The presence of Timothy and Sopater (Rom 16:21; cf. Acts 20:4)

G. Probably the letter was taken to Rome by Phoebe (16:1, 2).

PURPOSE OF WRITING

There are various possibilities. (See *CMM*, 250-252.)

A. To prepare for his visit with them.

1. Why was he coming?

- Wanted to impart some spiritual gift that he and they might be mutually edified (1:11, 12)
- Wanted to preach the gospel to them (1:15)
- Hoped to receive their support in the future (15:24)

2. What might the letter have accomplished?

- It would introduce him and the gospel he preached.
- It might answer some critics (3:8).

B. To teach the church:

- 15:14, 15
- 16:17, 18

- 14:1–15:13

C. Perhaps to put down his message about salvation in some kind of finished form, because of the possibility of trouble when he arrived in Jerusalem (15:30–32).

D. To help the church adjust to a situation in which Gentiles were in the majority and in positions of leadership, but Jews who had formerly been expelled from Rome were now returning to be part of the church.

CHARACTERISTICS AND CONTRIBUTION

A. Hiebert lists the following characteristics:

- Most formal of Paul's epistles.
- Its universalism.
- Systematic and logical arrangement of its contents.
- Language: great energy, but without vehemence.
- Profoundly doctrinal—but about salvation, not so much about Christ, or the church, or last things.
- More quotations from the Old Testament than in other epistles; someone said there were 61 Old Testament quotations from 14 different Old Testament books.

B. Great significance:

1. Throughout Christian history, it has been regarded as the cornerstone of Christian theology. Luther, e.g., is quoted as saying, "If you get Romans, God gets you." It is often

thought of more as a theological "treatise" or "tractate" than a letter.

2. Still, it cannot really be considered a "systematic theology."

C. It is interesting that

- Paul had very much wanted to go to Rome (Rom 15:22, 23) and
- Paul finally did get to go to Rome (Acts 23:11; 28:16), but
- not in the way he had planned.

Does this suggest something about how the providence of God may work in a Christian's (preacher's, missionary's) life?

TEXT

See *CMM*, 245–247; and Harrison, 307–311. Two main questions regard:

A. The placement of the doxology (16:25–27) at the end of the letter. A doxology is not typical of Paul's writing and various manuscripts include this one in different places. But it could be Paul's work.

B. The ending of the book—whether there was originally a fourteen-chapter or fifteen-chapter form of the book. See *CMM*, 245–247.

1. Some manuscripts end the book after only fourteen chapters.

- This has led to the thesis that perhaps the original letter was a tract intended to be used by the whole church and ended after chapter 14 and that the beginning and ending were added to individualize the letter for the church at Rome.
- It is more likely that someone—perhaps Marcion—abbreviated Paul's original letter by cutting off the last two chapters.

2. A fifteen-chapter book has been proposed, with the additional suggestion that chapter 16 was added when the letter was sent to Ephesus. Since Paul spent more time there than anywhere, it is argued, he would have known more people there. But there is no manuscript evidence for a 15-chapter book, and it is unlikely that one ever existed since the subject in chapter 14 is continued into chapter 15.

OUTLINE

See the outline by J. D. Thomas.

Outline of the Book of Romans
by J. D. Thomas*

DOCTRINAL SECTION (Chapters 1–8)

A. INTRODUCTION. (1:1–17)

- Author's salutation, prayer, and debt (1:1–15)
- The Theme: "Righteousness by the Gospel — Justification by Faith" (1:16, 17)

B. Condemnation (1:18–3:20) — "Righteousness Needed"

- Gentile condemnation (1:18–32) Idolatry, sensuality, immorality
- Principles by which God judges men (2:1–16)
- Jewish condemnation (2:17–29) (The same principles as the Gentiles.) Immorality: Do you steal? Sensuality: Do you commit adultery? Sacrilege: Do you rob temples?

- Jewish protests (3:1–8)
- Scriptures condemn Jews as well as Gentiles (3:9–20)

C. Justification (3:21–5:21) — "Righteousness Provided"

- Righteousness is apart from the law (3:21–31).
- Abraham's righteousness was reckoned according to faith (4:1–17a).
- The Christian's faith is like Abraham's in character (4:17b–25).
- Results of justification in Christ (5:1–11)
- Adam and Christ (5:12–21)

D. Sanctification (6–7) "Righteousness Experienced"

- Saints cannot continue in sin, because they are dead to it (6:1–14).
- They must not continue in sin, for they are under grace (6:15–20).
- The cost of sin is prohibitive (6:21–23).
- Christians are judicially dead to the Law (7:1–6).
- The Law served a good purpose, but Christ is the only hope (7:7–25).

E. Glorification (8) "Righteousness Gives Hope and Assurance"

- The new relationship is spiritual (8:1–11).
- Adoption and heirship (8:12–25)

- The assurance of salvation (8:26–39)

EXPLANATORY (Chapters 9–11)

(The righteousness of faith reconciled to: the promises made to Israel, the election of the people, and the faithfulness of God.)

A. Mourning for Israel (9:1–5)

B. Israel's rejection is not inconsistent with God's promise, which has been kept to all who continue to qualify (9:14–18).

C. Israel's rejection is not inconsistent with God's justice (9:14–18).

D. God's absolute power asserted: His justice and mercy vindicated; and His rejection of Israel in harmony with prophecy (9:19–29).

E. The Gentiles, following the law of *faith*, contrasted with the Jews, following the law of *works* (9:30–33).

F. The failure of the Jews to see that Christ was the termination and aim of the Law (10:1–13).

G. Righteousness comes by faith, and faith comes by hearing—to which Jews and Gentiles alike had equal opportunity (10:14–21).

H. The rejection of Israel is not total (11:1–10).

I. Israel's rejection is not final—the Gentiles are not to glory *over* Israel—they, too, can still receive mercy (11:11–32).

J. Ascriptions of praise for God's ways and judgments (11:33–36).

HORTATORY (12:1–15:13)

A. Self-dedication encouraged; self-conceit discouraged (12:1–8)

B. A catalog of virtues (12:9–21)

C. Concerning governments; love; and approaching salvation (13:1–14)

D. General exhortations (14:1–15:13)

CONCLUDING THOUGHTS

Salutations, Warnings, and Benedictions (15:14–16:25)

* * *

*With apologies to R. C. Bell, for Bible 398, Abilene Christian University, ca. 1958.

Notes on First Corinthians

AUTHOR

1 AND 2 CORINTHIANS ARE AMONG THE FOUR LETTERS of Paul (along with Romans and Galatians) which are almost universally accepted as being written by Paul.

CORINTH

A. Corinth is a city in the southern part of Greece, the capital of the Roman province of Achaia. "The city occupied a powerful position at the S. extremity of the narrow four-mile isthmus which connected the mainland of Greece with the Peloponnese" (Hastings *Dictionary of the Bible*).

B.

The wealthy and ancient city of Corinth was utterly destroyed by the Romans in 146 BC, and its citizens were killed or sold into slavery .... A century later Julius Caesar founded the city afresh, this time as a Roman colony, and from 29 BC on, it served as the seat of a proconsul and the capital of the senatorial province of Achaia (Carson, Moo, and Morris, 263).

It was the old city that had a notorious character; nevertheless, "as a great port city it is unlikely that new Corinth established a reputation for moral probity (see 1 Cor 6:12ff.)" (*CMM*, 263).

PAUL'S RELATIONSHIP TO THE CHURCH AT CORINTH

A. It is somewhat difficult to put all of Paul's dealings with the church at Corinth into a single context, to determine how all the various letters we have and various visits which he mentions can be put together into one narrative.

- For instance, we have two letters to Corinth. But Paul wrote at least one other (1 Cor 5:9). And he possibly, or probably, wrote another that we do not have a copy of (2 Cor 7:8). Thus, there were possibly, or probably, four letters from Paul to Corinth; *CMM* speaks of them as Corinthians A, B (1 Cor), C, D (2 Cor).
- Furthermore, we know of the visit Paul made to Corinth on the second missionary journey (Acts 18:1). But Acts does not record another visit there until Acts 20:2, 3. Yet Paul at some time made a "painful" visit there (2 Cor 2:1). Thus the visit to Corinth that he planned when he

wrote 2 Corinthians was to be his third visit there (2 Cor 12:14; 13:1).

B. The following is one attempt to put Paul's relationship to Corinth into the context of his missionary journeys.

1. On the second missionary journey, after leaving Luke at Philippi (Acts 16:40), and Silas and Timothy at Berea, Paul went on by himself to Athens (Acts 17:14).

2. After preaching at Athens (Acts 17:16–33), Paul went on to Corinth (Acts 18:1).

3. At Corinth he stayed with Priscilla and Aquila (who were also tentmakers), and worked with them as a tentmaker, supporting himself as he preached (Acts 18:2–4).

4. When Silas and Timothy came from Macedonia (Acts 18:5), Paul was able to quit working as a tentmaker and give his full time to preaching and teaching, apparently because he received support from the churches in Macedonia (See 2 Cor 11:9; 1 Thess 2:17–3:10).

5. In Corinth Paul felt afraid (2 Cor 2:3), and it was necessary for God to reassure him (Acts 18:9, 10).

6. Paul arrived in Corinth about AD 50 and preached there for 18 months (Acts 18:11). He established the church in Corinth (2 Cor 10:14). He must have had considerable success in the work there (Acts 18:8).

7. From Corinth he returned to Antioch to conclude the second missionary journey, traveling back by way of Ephesus, leaving Priscilla and Acquila at Ephesus, and promising to return there (Acts 18:19–21).

8. Before Paul returned to Ephesus, Apollos went there from Alexandria and was privately "straightened out" by Priscilla an,d Aquila. From there Apollos went on to Corinth

(Acts 18:24–19:1). From his stay in Corinth came the references in 1 Corinthians to Apollos (1 Cor 1:12; 3:6; 4:6).

9. On the third missionary journey. Paul spent most of his time in Ephesus. The journey began in about 53 (or a year or two earlier), and Paul, after traveling overland through Galatia and Phrygia, arrived in Ephesus in about 54. He preached in the synagogue for three months (Acts 19:8), then taught daily in the hall of Tyrannus for two years (Acts 19:10), and after that stayed even longer until he could say he had worked in Ephesus for three years (Acts 20:31). Thus, he was in Ephesus about 54–57. One of the first things he did there was to "rebaptize" twelve men who knew only John's baptism—presumably men who had been taught by Apollos during his stay at Ephesus (Acts 19:1–7).

10. From Ephesus Paul wrote the Corinthian church a letter, presumably about immorality and avoiding brethren who live in immorality. We do not have this letter (1 Cor 5:9). *CMM* calls it "Corinthians A."

11. Paul heard disturbing news about the church in Corinth from members of Chloe's household (1 Cor 1:11). Apparently they had traveled from Corinth to Ephesus with this news.

12. Perhaps at about the same time, three members of the church at Corinth arrived at Ephesus (1 Cor 16:17, 18); they may have brought a letter from the church asking Paul several questions. (1 Cor 7:1) They may also have communicated other information orally.

13. Paul speaks of Timothy's coming to the church in Corinth (1 Cor 4:17; 16:10). One possibility is that Paul was sending the letter, 1 Corinthians, with Timothy, as well as with the three brethren from Corinth. Another is that before

Paul responded in writing to Chloe's information, and before he answered the Corinthians' questions, he sent Timothy to Corinth, probably to try to "straighten out" the situation. Timothy may have left before the three messengers from Corinth arrived. However, he may have gone to Corinth by way of Macedonia (Acts 19:22), with the result that Paul anticipated that his letter to the church (1 Cor) would get there before Timothy did.

14. At the time that Chloe's people brought news and the three brothers from Corinth arrived, Paul wrote a letter to the church to try to answer the questions they had asked and to try to solve their problems. This is our First Corinthians. (*CMM*: Corinthians B) When Paul wrote it he was in Ephesus (1 Cor 16:8). It would have been written near the end of his time in Ephesus, thus about 56 or 57.

15. When he wrote First Corinthians, Paul planned to stay in Ephesus for a while longer (1 Cor 16:8, 9), then to go to Macedonia (1 Cor 16:5), then to spend some time in Corinth (1 Cor 16:6, 7) before going on to Jerusalem with the contribution for the saints (1 Cor 16:1–4; Acts 24:17).

16. Soon after, false apostles arrived in Corinth, apparently bearing letters of recommendation. (2 Cor 3:1; 10:12–18; 11:22, 23) They succeeded in gaining a large following.

17. Timothy arrived back in Ephesus (2 Cor 1:1), apparently with a bad report about the church in Corinth.

18. Paul made a quick trip to Corinth from Ephesus, but his visit there (his second visit to Corinth) was "painful," and thus unsuccessful (2 Cor. 2:1; 12:14; 13:1). (Some place this trip earlier.)

19. Paul, having told the Corinthians he would go back to Corinth before going to Macedonia (2 Cor 1:15, 16),

wrote a letter in lieu of that visit. This letter was written "with many tears" and out of "much affliction and anguish of heart" (2 Cor 2:4) and was carried to Corinth by Titus (2 Cor 2:12, 13; 7:5–7). This is another "lost letter." (*CMM*: Corinthians C) (Some think it may be 2 Cor 10–13; others see in 2 Cor. 2:4 a reference to 1 Cor.)

20. After the riot in Ephesus (Acts 19:23ff), Paul left Ephesus for Troas. He had arranged with Titus to meet him along a prearranged route. Paul hoped to see Titus at Troas but did not find him there (2 Cor 2:12, 13). Not finding Titus there, he went on to Macedonia.

21. Somewhere in Macedonia Titus met Paul with the report that the situation in Corinth had improved. Paul, along with Timothy, then sent a letter (our 2 Corinthians— *CMM*: Corinthians D), which is taken by Titus and two brothers (2 Cor. 8:16–23). They are to gather the Corinthian collection before Paul himself arrives in Corinth (2 Cor 9:3, 4). Paul was planning a visit shortly (2 Cor. 12:14; 13:1)—his third visit to Corinth.

22. Paul spent three months in Greece—probably in Corinth—before continuing on the journey to Jerusalem with which he concluded the third missionary journey (Acts 20:3). He went to Jerusalem to take the contribution to the poor saints. It is while he is in Corinth that he writes the letter to the Romans. Hiebert says, "The tranquil atmosphere of Romans reveals that the Corinthian troubles were successfully settled." (Hiebert, 147.)

C. Thus, 1 and 2 Corinthians were both written by Paul during the third missionary journey, near the end of that journey—1 Corinthians from Ephesus, about 56 (*CMM* estimates 55; Hiebert, 57) and 2 Corinthians a few months later from Macedonia. House (16), dates 1 Corinthians at 54 and 2 Corinthians at 55.

THE CONTENTS OF FIRST CORINTHIANS

A. Problem: Disunity and factionalism from following different preachers (1:10–12).

Solution: Get a clearer understanding of the role of the word and the preacher in God's plan.

- It's not by man's wisdom, but by God's, that we are saved.
- The preacher is nothing, compared to God, Who gives the harvest.
- It is ridiculous to boast and to be puffed up one against another.

B. Problem: Immorality in the church (ch. 5).

Solution: Drive out the wicked person (5:13) and shun immorality (6:18).

C. Problem: Christians 'going to law' against one another (6:1–8). Solution: Don't do it, but settle your problems among yourselves.

D. Problems: Related to marriage and divorce (ch. 7).

Solutions:

- If you are married, stay married.
- If you are not married, don't get married.
- If you marry, you do not sin.
- Marriage is God's way to prevent immorality.

- In marriage, each partner should meet the other's sexual needs.
- Widows may remarry under certain conditions.

E. Problem: Meat offered to idols (chs. 8–10).
Solution: Don't eat meat if it causes your brother to fall (8:13).

- Paul provides a good example of a brother who gave up his rights.
- In the Old Testament, the fathers provide a bad example of self-indulgence.

F. Problem: Related to worship: Woman's veiling (11:2–16).
Solution: Women should keep their heads covered while they pray and prophesy.

G. Problem: Related to worship: The Lord's Supper (11:17–33). Solution: Don't confuse the Lord's Supper with a fellowship meal. But recognize the seriousness of the occasion when you have the Lord's Supper.

H. Problem: Related to worship: Spiritual gifts, especially tongues (chs. 12–14).
Solutions:

- Recognize that God gives gifts to all and all gifts are important.
- See the superiority of love.
- Learn that prophecy is more valuable than tongues.

- Do everything decently and in order, especially in the use of tongues.

I. Problem: Related to worship: women speaking in church (14:33–35). Solution: Women should keep silent in the churches.

J. Problem: False doctrine concerning the resurrection (ch. 15). Solution:

- Remember that the doctrine of the resurrection is essential to the Christian faith.
- A better understanding of how we are resurrected will help clear up some problems.

K. Problem: Collection for the saints (16:1–4). Solution: Take up a regular contribution.

THEME OR PURPOSE

A. The primary purpose is to answer questions raised by the church (1 Cor 7:1) and to correct problems in the church made known by members of Chloe's household (1 Cor 1:11) and perhaps by others (1 Cor 16:17). It is also intended to prepare the church to give to help the poor saints in Jerusalem (1 Cor 16:1, 2). From this standpoint, its theme might be said to be: *Solutions to Church Problems.*

B. Most, if not all, of the problems can be related to the problem of disunity. Perhaps, then, the theme could be said to be: *Division: Symptoms and Cure.*

C. Black suggests that the unifying strand in all the problems is "life in a pagan society" (Allen Black, 12).

Notes on Second Corinthians

AUTHOR, DATE, PROVENANCE

SECOND CORINTHIANS WAS WRITTEN BY PAUL ABOUT 56 from Macedonia near the end of the third missionary journey a few months (or within a year) after Paul wrote First Corinthians from Ephesus, and not long before he wrote Romans from Corinth. There is little or no question that Paul in fact is the author of both the Corinthian epistles.

FIRST AND SECOND CORINTHIANS COMPARED

The First gives insight into the character and condition of the early churches; the Second, into the life and character of the Apostle Paul. The First is objective and practical; the Second is subjective and personal. The First is systematic; the Second is not. The First is deliberate; the Second is impassioned. The First warns against Pagan influences;

the Second, against Judaic influences. The two together are valuable beyond all estimate for an understanding of the problems of first century Christians, and for an appreciation of the greatest missionary of the Christian era. (W. Graham Scroggie, quoted in Hiebert, 152.)

BETWEEN FIRST AND SECOND CORINTHIANS

A. Second Corinthians speaks of a "painful visit" by Paul (2:1). When did this occur? Paul was about to go there for the third time (12:14; 13:1). But this "third visit" is undoubtedly that mentioned in Acts 20:2, 3. Since his first visit with the Corinthians would have been the occasion on which he established the church there (Acts 18), we must conclude that his second visit, this "painful visit," is not recorded in Acts, and must have occurred during Paul's three-year ministry in Ephesus on the third missionary tour.

B. Second Corinthians also speaks of a "sorrowful letter" (2:3–11; 7:11, 12). What was this letter? According to Black, 13:

- It has been equated with 1 Corinthians. This view is not generally accepted now, largely because "the offense against Paul in the sorrowful letter was personal as seen in 2:5, 10 and 7:11, 12." 1 Corinthians, in contrast, addressed many other issues.
- It was a letter which has been lost. This is the most widely accepted theory today.
- "II Corinthians 10–13 is the sorrowful letter and was redacted into II Corinthians. This is of

course possible only if 10–13 is viewed as separable from II Corinthians." Furthermore, 2 Corinthians 10–13 doesn't fit the description of the letter mentioned in 2 Corinthians 2 and 7.

C. Thus, it seems reasonable to conclude that between 1 Corinthians and 2 Corinthians, there was a "painful visit" and a "sorrowful letter," and that that "sorrowful letter" has been lost to us. (Thus, Paul apparently wrote four letters to the Corinthians.)

TEXT

The integrity of the text:

A. The major question regarding the integrity of the Corinthian letters has to do with 2 Corinthians 10–13, which is held to be too different from 2 Corinthians 1–9 to be a part of the same letter. Four possible solutions to this problem are suggested by Carson, Moo, and Morris, 267–272:

- The view that 2 Corinthians 10–13 is the severe and painful letter mentioned in the earlier chapters of the book. See *CMM*, 268, 269.
- 2 Corinthians was written at one time. "Certainly this coheres with the textual evidence." (*CMM*, p. 269) The differences between the two sections of the letter are exaggerated.
- 2 Corinthians 10–13 make up another letter written after 2 Corinthians 1–9. It would then

be Paul's fifth letter (Corinthians E) to the church at Corinth. How did one lose its greeting and the other its conclusion?

- 2 Corinthians 10–13 is a part of the same letter but written at a different, slightly later time. This is the view favored by *CMM*.

B. Other, less serious, questions are raised about:

- 2 Corinthians 2:14–7:4;
- 2 Corinthians 6:14–7:1;
- 2 Corinthians 8, 9.

THE MAJOR PURPOSE OF SECOND CORINTHIANS

To establish Paul's authority.

A. Why was Paul concerned about establishing his authority?

- It was *not* just an ego trip!
- Rather, it was for the good of the Corinthians. See 2 Corinthians 11:2; 12:14, 15; 12:19–21; 13:7.
- At stake was an essential principle: the question of apostolic authority. Notice how often Paul speaks of authority in 2 Corinthians: (a) 2:17; (b) 3:5, (c) 4:1, 2; (d) 4:5-7; (e) 5:9–14; (f) 6:1, 4; (g) 5:18–20; (h) 10:7, 8; (i) 10:13; (j) 10:18; (k) 11:5; (l) 12:12; (m) 13:3; (n) 13:10.

B. How does Paul achieve his purpose?

1. He exposes the "rascals" who oppose him.

- 2:17 — apparently Paul speaks of them as "peddlers"
- 3:1ff — apparently they had letters of recommendation
- 10:12 — they commended themselves
- 11:4 — they preach a different gospel
- 11:5 — with sarcasm, he calls them "superlative" apostles
- 11:12 — they claimed to work on the same basis as Paul
- 11:13 — they were false apostles, deceitful workmen, disguised as apostles of Christ
- 1:15 — they were servants of Satan
- 11:18 — they boasted of worldly things
- 11:19 — they were fools
- 11:20 — they made fools of others
- 11:21ff — apparently they made great claims about being Jews, belonging to Christ, suffering for Christ (?), etc.
- 12:12 — apparently they did *not* do the signs of a true apostle

2. He answers their charges.

- They apparently claimed that Paul was fickle (1:17).
- They apparently claimed that Paul used cunning with a veiled gospel (1:15—2:4).

- They may have claimed that Paul bragged about himself, or that he pretended to have too much authority; and they may have accused him of having no letters of recommendation, as they had (3:1 ff).
- They apparently said that Paul had no position, and may have said that he was mad (5:12, 13).
- Paul's emphasis on his trials and difficulties (1:8; 4:8ff; 4:16ff; 6:4ff; et al.) perhaps suggests that he was being criticized as a troublemaker.
- They may have been criticizing Paul's administration of the money being taken up for the poor saints (8:16–24).
- They apparently criticized Paul because he was imposing and bold in his letters, but weak face-to-face (10:1, 9, 10).
- They suspected Paul of acting in a worldly fashion (10:2).
- They seem to have claimed that Paul was not one of the original apostles and was not therefore worthy to be heard (12:12).
- Apparently, they held that Paul was to be blamed because he had not been supported in Corinth, but had supported himself (11:7ff).

OTHER PURPOSES OF SECOND CORINTHIANS

A. To define, explain, and defend the ministry carried on by Paul and others.

B. To exhort the Corinthians (a) to have the same feelings for Paul that he had for them, and (b) to abstain from being linked with unbelievers.

C. To prepare the Corinthians to give the contribution to the poor saints.

SOME CHARACTERISTICS OF SECOND CORINTHIANS

A. It is the most autobiographical of Paul's epistles. It reveals the following about him that we do not know from any other source:

1. The problem in Asia he speaks of in 1:8ff. (Could this have to do with the riot in Acts 19?)

2. The visit he speaks of in 2:1, 2.

3. The visit to Troas he speaks of in 2:12ff.

4. The problems at Macedonia in 7:5 and his meeting with Titus in 7:6.

5. The fact that in some way his physical appearance or presence was weak (or that because of it he could be accused of being weak), and that even his speaking ability could be criticized (10:10 and 11:6).

6. (The fact that Paul was determined to be a spiritual "pioneer"—a missionary—is revealed in 10:15, 16, but this is also known from Romans.)

7. The fact that Paul received support from other churches to preach at Corinth (11:8, 9).

8. Details about Paul's escape from Damascus (11:32, 33).

9. The list of trials and suffering is given in 11:21–29.

10. Paul's vision is described in 12:1–4.

11. Paul's thorn in the flesh (12:7ff).

B. It contains some of the best information in the New Testament concerning the work of a minister.

C. It also contains some memorable passages.

- 1:3–7 and 7:6, 7 — the emphasis on comfort
- 3:3 — we are epistles
- 3:7–18 — the contrast between two covenants
- 4:5–7 — the treasure in earthen vessels
- 4:16–5:10 — the inner and outer man, heaven, judgment
- 5:11 — we persuade men
- 5:17–21 — the ministry of reconciliation
- 6:2 — now is the accepted time
- 6:14ff — do not be mismated with unbelievers
- 8 and 9 — instructions regarding giving
- 10:12 — don't compare yourself with others
- 13:5 — examine yourselves

AN OUTLINE OF THE CONTENTS OF SECOND CORINTHIANS

A. Salutation and opening prayer (1:1–7).

B. News and personal defense (1:8–2:13).

C. Paul's explanation and vindication of his and Timothy's ministry (2:14–7:4)

1. Where our ministry came from: We were commissioned by God. (2:17) Therefore:

- We do not need letters of commendation.
- We are confident.
- We are bold.

- We do not lose heart in the face of rejection.
- We do not lose heart in the face of affliction.

2. What our ministry consists of:

- We persuade men.
- We have a work of reconciliation.
- We beseech you: be reconciled to God.

3. How our ministry affects you:

- We exhort you: do not accept God's grace in vain.
- Be as concerned for us as we are for you.
- Do not be yoked with unbelievers, but cleanse yourselves.

D. News and personal defense, continued (7:5–16).

E. Instructions concerning the collection for the saints (Chs. 8, 9).

F. Paul's defense of his apostleship (10:1–13:10).

G. Final words (13:11–14).

Notes on Galatians

AUTHOR

PAUL. NO ONE QUESTIONS PAUL'S AUTHORSHIP.

ADDRESSEES, DATE, PROVENANCE

"Churches of Galatia." But who were they? This is the crux of Galatians, although it does not affect the interpretation of the letter.

A. Also mentioned in 1 Corinthians 16:1.

B. There are two theories:

1. The "Northern Galatia" theory.

- This is the area in northern modern-day Turkey (north central Asia Minor) where the Gauls first settled. This would be the home of the "ethnic" Galatians.

- Did Paul ever visit this region? Possibly he did, as mentioned in Acts 16:6, on the second missionary journey, and 18:23, on the third journey. But if he did we know nothing about his experiences there except what may be implied in the letter.

2. The "Southern Galatia" theory.

- This is the area in south central Turkey that was included in the Roman province of Galatia. These "Galatians" then would not have been "ethnic" Galatians, but Galatians in the sense that they inhabited a territory that was part of a political entity known as "Galatia."
- This is the area that Paul first visited on his first missionary journey which included the cities of Antioch, Iconium, and Derbe (Acts 13, 14); he visited the area again on the second journey and on the third. Acts 16:6 and 18:23 in that case would not refer to northern Galatia but to "Phrygian-Galiatian" and would include the area where Paul established churches on his first missionary journey.

C. There are arguments for and against both viewpoints. House, 136–139.

D. While the interpretation of Galatians is not affected by which of the theories one accepts, the chronology of Paul's life and letters is, as is the interpretation of Acts.

1. If the Northern Galatia theory is accepted, then Gala-

tians was written sometime during or after the third missionary journey, because 4:13 may imply that Paul had preached there more than once. This would make the date about the mid–50s.

2. If the Southern Galatia theory is accepted, then Galatians was written after the first missionary journey because Paul visited the churches twice on that journey. In this case, Galatians would probably be the earliest of Paul's letters.

3. In Galatians Paul mentions two visits to Jerusalem (1:18; 2:1). In Acts Paul mentions three visits to Jerusalem (Acts 9:26–30; 11:30; 15).

- It is hard (perhaps not impossible) to reconcile these two facts if one accepts the Northern Galatia theory. The Jerusalem conference is in this case equated with the visit described in Galatians 2.

- If one accepts the Southern Galatia theory, the visit to Jerusalem mentioned in Galatians 2 is to be equated with the visit to Jerusalem mentioned in Acts 11. The third visit in Acts, for the Jerusalem conference, is not mentioned in Galatians because it had not yet occurred. If this theory is true, Galatians can be dated at the end of the first missionary journey and just before the Jerusalem conference (perhaps during the time spoken of in Acts 14:28), or probably about 48 or 49.

E. Which of the two theories one accepts will determine both the date he assigns to the letter and its place of writing.

SITUATION AND PURPOSE

A. Paul's relationship to the churches:

- It was because of an infirmity that he first preached to them (4:14).
- They felt great goodwill towards him (4:16).
- Paul considered them his children; he cared greatly for them (4:19).
- Paul is very disturbed about their acceptance of false teaching. He does not, for instance, include a prayer for their spiritual welfare at the beginning of the letter.

B. False teachers (Judaizing teachers) had come into the churches, teaching that it was necessary for Gentiles to be circumcised before they could be saved. See Galatians 1:6–9; 5:7–12; 5:2–4; 6:12. This was the "other gospel" which they taught. Notice that the question was not whether it was all right for Jews to be circumcised. Circumcision by itself meant nothing. Galatians 5:6.

C. They may have also tried to enforce other requirements of the law (Gal 4:10; 4:21).

D. It is possible that, in addition, these Judaizers were criticizing Paul (Gal 1:10).

E. Paul fought against their false understanding by teaching that the Galatians had not been saved by works of the law, but by faith (Gal 2:15, 16); indeed, the law had been taken away, and they were now free from the law (Gal 3:23–25).

F. However, they needed to make sure they did not exercise their freedom irresponsibly. They still lived under law (Gal 6:2) and they were still obligated to live in a certain way (Gal 5:16ff).

OUTLINE from Black, 9.

A. Greetings — note foreshadowing of concerns (1:1–5).

B. Paul's judgment on the false gospel. Note: no prayer, but Paul goes directly to rebuke (1:6–9).

C. Autobiographical defense of apostleship and gospel (1:10–2:14).

D. Theological arguments against the Judaizers (2:15–5:12).

- Appeal to Galatians' experience of salvation; not via works but by faith.
- Appeal to scripture showing "promise" was based on faith rather than on keeping the law of Moses.

E. Both arguments raise the question of a license to sin; therefore, ...

F. Restrictions on Christian freedom (5:13–6:10).

G. Closing (6:11–18).

IMPORTANCE

Galatians has been universally hailed as extremely important for the understanding of Christianity. It has been called the "Magna Carta of Christian Liberty."

Notes on the Prison Epistles

WHAT ARE THE PRISON EPISTLES?

THE PRISON EPISTLES ARE EPHESIANS, PHILIPPIANS, Colossians, and Philemon. Sometimes called "captivity" or "imprisonment" epistles.

A. Why are they called "prison epistles"? Because Paul refers to himself as a prisoner when he writes all three. See: Ephesians 3:1; 4:1; 6:20; Philippians 1:12–14; Colossians 4:3, 18; Philemon 9, 10, 13. (Paul was also in prison in 2 Timothy.)

B. There are other close connections between three of these books.

- Colossians and Ephesians are very similar. "Of the 155 verses in Ephesians it is estimated that 73 have verbal parallels in Colossians." (Weed, *The Letters of Paul to the Ephesians, Colossians, and Philemon,* 111.)

- Ephesians mentions Tychicus (Eph 6:21). Colossians also mentions Tychicus (Col 4:7, 8, 9). And Colossians mentions Onesimus, who is mentioned in Philemon. Paul says in Philemon that he is sending Onesimus back to Philemon (Phlm 12).
- Thus, it would appear that Ephesians, Colossians, and Philemon were all written about the same time, and were possibly all "mailed" at the same time—carried by Tychicus to the recipients.

C. Philippians doesn't have this close relationship to the other epistles that they have to one another, but it too was written from prison.

FROM WHERE AND WHEN WERE THE PRISON EPISTLES WRITTEN?

A. According to Harrison, three places have been suggested: Ephesus (Acts 19), Caesarea (Acts 24:27), and Rome (Acts 28:30, 31). See the discussion in Harrison, 315–321.

B. Harrison concludes that the letters to Ephesians, Colossians, and Philemon were written "around the middle of the sojourn in Rome, and Philippians shortly after the close of the two-year period" (322).

C. Carson, Moo, and Morris point out that there are two times and places when Paul was definitely in prison—in Caesarea for two years (Acts 23:33; 24:27) and in Rome for two years (Acts 28:16ff). But they also note that these were not his only imprisonments. See 2 Corinthians 11:3 and the evidence from 1 Clement.

- Ephesus has been suggested as one place where he may have been imprisoned. See 2 Corinthians 11:23; 1 Corinthians 15:32; 2 Corinthians 1:8–11. *CMM* seem to favor Ephesus as the place from which Philippians was written (319–321). This would have occurred on the third missionary journey.
- They seem to favor Rome (about AD 60–62) as the provenance for the other three prison epistles (*CMM*, 334, 335).

Notes on Ephesians

THE RELATIONSHIP BETWEEN EPHESIANS AND COLOSSIANS

A. THESE TWO EPISTLES ARE VERY MUCH ALIKE. THEY not only deal with many of the same subjects, but they use much of the same language.

B. The same person, Tychicus, was apparently the person who carried both letters to the recipients (Cf. Eph 6:21, 22 and Col 4:7, 8).

C. How are they related? It is usually thought that Colossians was written first by Paul and that Paul then used Colossians in the writing of Ephesians or else that Paul simply had some of the same things in mind when he wrote Ephesians.

SOME HAVE QUESTIONED PAUL'S AUTHORSHIP OF EPHESIANS

A. Arguments against Pauline authorship have been based on the letter's relationship to Colossians, on style and language (e.g., the sentences are longer in Ephesians), and on a supposed lack of acquaintance with the readers.

B. The supposed lack of acquaintance proves nothing; the relationship to Colossians can be accounted for otherwise; and the differences in style and language are not enough to outweigh the evidence of Paul's authorship.

C. In favor of Paul's authorship: The letter claims to have been written by Paul; there's a very early tradition that he was the author; and much of the style, language, structure, and theology is like Paul (Black, 22).

THERE IS A QUESTION AS TO WHETHER THE LETTER WAS ACTUALLY WRITTEN TO THE CHURCH AT EPHESUS

A. Why?

1. The question arises because "in Ephesus" is not included in the best manuscripts (not in the RSV, but it is in the NRSV) in Ephesians 1:1.

- Therefore, if the expression is not in the text, all we have to go on is the heading: "To the Ephesians." This is a very old heading that reflects the belief of those in the church from an early age.

- But the heading itself does not prove that this was a personal epistle written to the church in Ephesus.

2. In addition, it is argued that since the letter is quite impersonal and formal, it is not the kind of letter that Paul would have written to a church where he had labored for three years (Acts 20:31) and where he must have had many beloved friends.

- Ephesians can be contrasted with Romans. Paul had worked long in Ephesus but mentions no one. He had never been to Rome but mentioned everyone.
- But who is to say that Paul must address a certain number of people by name for the letter to be to a certain place?

3. Furthermore, one of the earliest witnesses to the canon, the heretic Marcion, includes Ephesians but calls it the "Letter to the Laodiceans" (see Col. 4:16). Apparently his copy of the letter did not indicate who were the recipients and he assumed from Colossians that it was the otherwise lost letter referred to in Colossians 4.

B. If not to Ephesus, then to whom?

- One theory, proposed by Goodspeed, suggested that Ephesians was a letter written by a "Paulinist" who made a collection of Paul's letters and then wrote Ephesians in the style of Paul to provide an introduction to the entire body of Paul's work. For a discussion of this view, see *CMM*, 310, 311; Harrison, 337–339.

- Another explanation for the impersonal tone of the letter is that it may have been a "circular letter" intended to be circulated among the churches of Asia. Paul's letters were shared or circulated among the churches—see Colossians 4:16. Since Ephesus was the chief city of Asia, very early the name of Ephesus was attached to the letter.

C. There is not, of course, any insurmountable difficulty in believing that the letter was actually written to the church in Ephesus.

THE CITY OF EPHESUS WAS AN IMPORTANT CITY

A. It was located in Asia, a province in Asia Minor. See the seven churches of Asia in Revelation.

B. It was the most important city in Asia, being the great commercial center of Asia Minor—one of the three great trading centers in the eastern Mediterranean (along with Alexandria and Antioch). It prided itself on being the commercial and religious metropolis of Asia.

C. It was especially important as a center for the worship of the Greek and Roman Goddess Diana (or, in Greek, Artemis). There was a magnificent temple erected to this goddess in Ephesus. See Acts 19:27.

D. Ephesus was also a center of magic and of the use of sorcery. See Acts 19:18, 19.

WE KNOW MUCH ABOUT THE CHURCH IN EPHESUS

A. Paul visited there at the end of the second missionary journey (Acts 18:20, 21).

B. There Priscilla and Acquila taught Apollos (Acts 18:24–26).

C. There Paul spent most of the third missionary journey (Acts 19).

- There Paul encountered the twelve disciples who were "re-baptized" (19:1–7).
- There Paul preached in the synagogue for three months (19:8, 9).
- There Paul preached in the hall of Tyrannus for two years (19:10).
- From there the gospel spread throughout the area (19:10).
- There Paul performed extraordinary miracles (19:11, 12).
- There the sons of Sceva attempted to imitate Paul's miracles (19:13–17).
- There the books were burned (19:18–20).
- There the riot of the silversmiths occurred (19:23–41).
- Paul again visited with the Ephesian elders, meeting with them at Miletus, on his way back to Jerusalem at the end of the third journey (Acts 20:17–38).

D. In Rome(?) Paul writes to the Ephesian church from

prison (Acts 28:30).

E. Paul may have visited Ephesus again later after he was released from prison (See Hiebert, 257, and 1 Tim 1:3, 20).

F. The final mention we have of Ephesus is found in Revelation 2:1–7.

HOWEVER, EPHESIANS ITSELF REVEALS LITTLE ABOUT THE CHURCH

A. The letter is rather formal and impersonal. Paul does not include personal greetings, nor does he use the personal pronoun "I" as often in Ephesians as he does, for example, in Philippians. (This illustrates that the epistles were more than just letters. This is an essay as much as a letter.)

B. Furthermore, Paul does not speak to specific problems —either doctrinal or moral—as he does in his letters to Corinth, Galatia, and Colossae.

C. It is difficult, therefore, to single out an issue, or a controversy, that called forth the message of Ephesians.

WHAT THEN IS THE BOOK ABOUT? WHAT IS ITS THEME, PURPOSE, OR MAIN IDEA?

A. Black says that the purpose of Ephesians is to "encourage recent converts from a pagan background to live faithfully in a pagan society" (Black, 22).

B. Other answers might be given. It has been suggested that Ephesians 1:9, 10 summarizes the theme of the book as well as any verse. Every part of this passage is important.

- God had a purpose (1:5, 11; 3:11, 12; 3:9, 10).

- This purpose was centered in Christ (1:3–5; 1:19).
- This purpose was to unite "all things" in Him. Specifically, He united Jews and Gentiles (2:14–22).
- Once that purpose was hidden; it was a "mystery" (3:4, 5; 3:9).
- But now that mystery has been revealed (3:1–6).

C. Another way of looking at the book is to say that the theme of the book is unity:

UNITY: THE THEME OF EPHESIANS

I. Ephesians 1–3: The Theory of Unity: We are all one in Christ.

II. Ephesians 4–6: The Practice of Unity

- Unity of spirit (4:1–3)
- Unity of doctrine (4:4–6)
- Unity in work (4:7–16)
- Unity through right behavior (4:17–5:20)
- Unity in relationships (5:21–6:9)
- Unity in warfare (6:10–20)

D. It might also be said that the book is about the church and its part in the scheme of redemption. Ephesians could even be taken as a tract, or homily, on the church and its importance and part in God's plan. It may be that there was a need for such teaching because some saw Christianity as a solitary thing, and saw no need for the "togetherness" that the church involves. Notice what the book says about the church:

- The church is the fullness of Christ (1:20–22)
- We are reconciled to Christ in the body. (The church) (2:16)
- Gentiles and Jews are members of the same body (3:6)
- The church has a part to play in the eternal purpose of God (3:8–10)
- Glory is to be given to God in and through the church (3:20, 21)
- There is one church (4:4)
- Gifts are given to build up the church (4:11–16)
- Christ and the church are inseparable! (5:21–32)

AN OUTLINE OF EPHESIANS

A. From *Harper Study Bible*:

- Salutation — 1:1, 2
- Doctrinal affirmations — 1:3–3:21
- Practical exhortations — 4:1–6:20
- Conclusion — 6:21–24

B. From Black, 23:

- Greeting — 1:1–2
- The Blessings Received in Christ — 1:3–3:21
- Living Worthily of Those Blessings — 4:1–6:20
- Concluding Remarks — 6:21–24

C. This is typical of Paul. He generally includes something which gives the practical consequences of the doctrine he presents.

OTHER IMPORTANT DOCTRINES TAUGHT IN EPHESIANS

A. Some things seem to receive a special emphasis in Ephesians:

- The "heavenlies." ("Heavenly places")
- "Mystery."
- "God's eternal purpose."

B. Some other important teachings in Ephesians:

- Our salvation is according to plan — 1:3–10
- We are saved by grace — 2:5–10
- A remarkable change has occurred in the lives of those who are Christians — 2:11–13
- Unity is important — 4:4–6. See above.
- The church is important. See above.
- The relationship of husband and wife is regulated by God. See ch. 5.
- The relationship between parents and children is regulated by God. See ch. 6.
- The relationship between master and slave is regulated by God. See ch. 6.
- The Christian's warfare requires the "whole armor of God." — 6:10–17.

Notes on Philippians

AUTHOR, PROVENANCE, DATE

A. The letter claims to have been written by Paul. This is generally accepted.

B. For the place from which the letter was written, see the outline on the prison epistles.

- Usually, it is assumed that the letter was written from Rome, especially because of the mention of the Praetorian Guard (1:13) and Caesar's household (4:22). However, both of these existed outside Rome (Black, 18).
- Other possibilities are Caesarea and Ephesus. (Paul was also imprisoned in Philippi, but his stay there was too short to be relevant to the writing of this letter.)

C. The date depends on the place. If from Rome, it would have been written sometime between 60 and 62.

CLASSIFICATION

A. Philippians is classified as one of the prison epistles because Paul indicates in the letter that he is a prisoner (1:7, 13, 14, 17).

B. However, Philippians has less in common with the other three prison epistles than they have with each other.

- Ephesians mentions Tychicus, probably as the person who carried the letter (Eph 6:21, 22). Colossians also mentions Tychicus, in much the same way (Col 4:7, 8). The contents of Ephesians and Colossians are very similar.
- Colossians says that Paul is sending Onesimus (Col 4:10). Philemon was written to persuade Philemon to accept Onesimus back and specifies that Paul is sending him back (Phlm 12).
- With Paul when he wrote Colossians was Timothy (1:1), along with Aristarchus, Mark, Jesus Justus, Epaphras, Luke, and Demas (4:10–14). With Paul when he wrote Philemon were Timothy, Mark, Aristarchus, Demas, and Luke.
- There is a message for Archippus (linked with instructions concerning the church at Laodicea) in Colossians 4:12 and Philemon is addressed, in part, to Archippus (Phlm 2).

C. In contrast, the only thing Philippians has in common

with the others is that in Philippians Paul is in prison (and, in common with two of the others, Timothy is with him).

THE CITY OF PHILIPPI

A. Was the first city in Europe to hear the gospel, a Roman colony in the province of Macedonia.

B. *The New Smith's Bible Dictionary*:

a city of Macedonia, located approximately nine miles from the sea and some ten to twelve miles from its port Neapolis. Philip II of Macedon annexed the area (356 B.C.) which included the town; he afterward enlarged its borders and called it by his own name. In 168 B.C., Philippi became the property of the Romans (299).

PAUL AND THE CHURCH AT PHILIPPI

A. The letter was written by Paul (and Timothy) to the church in Philippi (1:1).

B. What had been Paul's relationship with that church?

1. About AD 49 (according to Black), he was first called to preach there when he was at Troas on the second missionary journey (Acts 16:8–10). Silas (Acts 15:40), Timothy (Acts 16:3ff), and Luke (Acts 16:10) accompanied him.

2. In Philippi, he converted Lydia and her household and cast the spirit of divination out of a slave-girl with the result that he and Silas were thrown into jail. They were freed by an earthquake and the conversion of the jailer and his family followed (16:16–34).

3. Paul and Silas were released by the magistrates and continued on the second missionary journey, apparently leaving Luke and Timothy there (Acts 17:4; 18:5; 20:5).

4. Near the end of the third missionary journey (which Paul spent mostly in Ephesus) he visited Macedonia twice (Acts 20:1, 3), sailing eventually from Philippi for Troas on his journey back to Jerusalem (20:5, 6).

5. Paul commended the churches in Macedonia (which would have included Philippi) for their liberal gifts to help the poor saints in Jerusalem (2 Cor 8:1–5).

6. The book of Philippians indicates that the church at Philippi had a long history of helping Paul:

- They had shared in the gospel "from the first day until now" (1:5, 7).
- Even when Paul went into Thessalonica they assisted him (4:15, 16ff).
- Recently, they had sent again to help him (4:10ff), a gift delivered by Epaphroditus (4:18).

C. What was the occasion for the writing of the book?

1. Paul wanted to thank the church for their help (Phil 1:3).

2. Paul wanted the brethren to know of his situation (Phil 1:12–26).

a. Paul was in prison. (See above.)

b. But his being in prison had resulted in more good being done (1:12–18).

- Some had been converted who would otherwise not have been converted (1:12, 13; see also 4:22).

- Some brethren had been made bolder in preaching (1:14).
- Others (apparently Paul's detractors, but who nevertheless preached the gospel) were also apparently preaching more boldly, with the result that Paul rejoiced (1:15–18).

c. Paul said that he might live or die, but believed that in either case God would be glorified (1:19–25).

d. But he was fairly sure that he would live and see the church again (1:19, 25, 26).

2. Paul wanted the church to know about Epaphroditus.

- Epaphroditus had brought a gift from Philippi to Paul (4:10, 18)
- Epaphroditus became ill; in fact, he almost died (2:26–30)
- The church at Philippi had heard about this and was concerned about the illness of Epaphroditus (2:25, 26).
- Epaphroditus had heard that the church at Philippi was concerned about him, and so he was distressed about their concern (2:25, 26).
- Therefore, Paul was eager to send Epaphroditus to Philippi, so that not only Epaphroditus and the Philippians might no longer be anxious, but also so that he (Paul) might no longer be anxious (2:28.)

THE MESSAGE OF PHILIPPIANS

A. Philippians is a "love letter," a "thank you" letter, a very personal letter from Paul to a church to which he felt very close.

B. Philippians contains little in the way of rebuke, but it does deal with various problems that the church at Philippi had experienced or was likely to experience.

- A doctrinal problem: false teachers (3:2ff).
- A practical problem: disunity (4:2; 2:1–11).

C. Philippians emphasizes joy; it includes the Greek word for "joy" or "rejoice" 14 times. Nine times as a verb — 1:18; 1:19; 2:17; 2:18 (a similar word is also found twice in 2:17, 18); 2:28; 3:1; 4:4 (two times); 4:10. Five times as a noun — 1:4; 1:25; 2:2; 2:29; 4:1.

ISSUES

A. Some believe that the letter as we have it is a composite of at least two other letters, especially because the word "finally" is used in 3:1. But "the same Greek phrase is also used in 1 Thessalonians 4:1 and 2 Thessalonians 3:1 and in each of these cases can be translated 'furthermore' or 'and so'" (Black, 17).

B. It is believed that 2:6–11 is an early Christian hymn. If so, Paul might have (1) composed the hymn, or (2) used a hymn by someone else to make his point. Another view is that others might have added it later.

- Other hymns in the New Testament: Colossians 1:15–20; Ephesians 5:14; Romans 11:33; 1 Timothy 3:16; 6:15–16; several in Revelation (Black, 17).
- To a great extent, all this is speculation. At any rate, it does not necessarily affect either the question of authorship or the interpretation of the passage.

Notes on Colossians

AUTHOR, DATE, PROVENANCE

A. PAUL (WITH TIMOTHY) IDENTIFIES HIMSELF AS THE author.

1. His authorship has been questioned by some on the grounds that

- the "vocabulary and sentence structure differ from the undisputed Pauline books,"
- the letter opposes gnosticism but full-blown gnosticism did not come into being until the second century,
- the author himself is gnostic to a degree (Black, 19).

2. None of these arguments carries much weight, and there is considerable external evidence that Paul is the author; there is also much evidence that the author of

Philemon also wrote Colossians. (Paul's authorship of Philemon is uncontested.)

B. The date depends on the place from which the letter was written. If it was written from Rome during Paul's imprisonment (Acts 28), then it would have been written about 60–62.

CLASSIFICATION

A. Colossians is one of the prison epistles, along with Ephesians, Philippians, and Philemon. Paul is in prison when he writes to the church in Colossae (4:4, 18).

B. Apparently, Tychicus carried Ephesians and Colossians, as well as Philemon, to the recipients of those letters, and he was apparently accompanied by Onesimus (Col 4:7; Eph 6:21).

C. Colossians and Philemon seem to be closely related; for the most part, the same people are with Paul and Timothy when both letters are written (Col 4:10–14; Phlm 23, 24), and Onesimus is mentioned in both (Phlm 10–12; Col 4:9).

CONTEXT

A. "Colossae was a town of Phrygia in Asia Minor, not far from Ephesus." (Notes from *The New Oxford Annotated Bible*, NRSV) It was near Laodicea and Hierapolis (Col 2:1; 4:13, 15, 16). "Colossae was located in the Lycus valley, in the province of Asia, some one hundred miles east of the capital city of Ephesus . . . Colossae had at one time been the

most important of the three cities but it had declined."
(Notes, *Harper Study Bible*, RSV)

B. Paul had never visited Colossae. (In this respect
Colossians is like Romans.)

- They had learned the gospel from Epaphras,
  who told Paul about their love (1:5–7).
- Paul had constantly prayed for them (1:9).
- But Paul had never seen them face to face (2:1).

C. It may be that the church at Colossae was established
during Paul's ministry in Ephesus on the third missionary
journey (Acts 19:9, 10). If so, Epaphras may have been
Paul's convert and/or student.

D. Paul wrote the church especially to counteract false
teaching which was bothering the church. Epaphras, who
had begun the church in Colossae—and who had also
worked with the churches in Laodicea and Hierapolis, was
with Paul when he wrote (4:12, 13).

E. He sent the letter by Tychicus, who was accompanied
by Onesimus. Apparently, they also carried the letters to
Ephesians and Philemon. In addition, there was a letter to
the Laodiceans (4:15–17). (Could this have been either
"Ephesians" or Philemon?)

PURPOSE(S)

A. One thing Paul wanted to accomplish through the (taking
of the) letter was to provide news about his work (maybe also
about Epaphras?) (4:7–9).

B. Paul also wanted by the same means to encourage the Colossians (4:8).

C. Primarily Paul's aim was to counteract false teaching —the "Colossian heresy": "I am saying this so that no one may deceive you with plausible arguments" (2:4). It appears that the particular false teaching bothering the Colossians was a syncretism, involving a combination of elements of early Gnosticism and Judaism. For a description, see 2:8ff:

- "Philosophy and empty deceit, according to human tradition, according to the elemental spirits of the universe, and not according to Christ" (2:8).
- "Matters of food and drink, observing festivals, new moons, sabbaths" (2:16).
- "Self-abasement, worship of angels, visions, puffed up without cause by a human way of thinking, and not holding fast to the head" (2:18, 19).
- Submitting to regulations, which have "an appearance of wisdom in promoting self-imposed piety, humility, and severe treatment of the body" (2:20–23).

MESSAGE, THEME

A. The theme of Colossians is the preeminence of Christ (Col 1:15–19).

B. The superiority of Christ is applied in a practical way to the problems faced by the church:

- Doctrinal issues: Since Christ is superior, there's no need for the intermediaries of the Gnostic system. And He is the fulfillment of the "mystery."
- Practical problems: Since Christ is superior and Christians are related to Christ, they need to live in a certain way.

OUTLINE

The following outline is from Black, 20.

- Greetings and prayer — 1:1–14
- Superiority of Christ (1:15–20 is the heart of the letter) — 1:15–2:7
- Superiority of Christ applied against false teachers — 2:8–23
- Superiority of Christ applied to everyday living — 3:1–4:6
- Concluding remarks — 4:7–18

Notes on the Thessalonian Epistles

AUTHOR

PAUL, ASSOCIATES SILAS (SILVANUS) AND TIMOTHY WITH him in the introduction to the letter. This suggests that the letters had to have been written during the second missionary journey, for Silas was not with Paul after that.

PRIMARY CHARACTERISTICS OF THESE LETTERS

A. These were among the first letters that Paul wrote. They were probably written from Corinth on the second missionary journey, only months after Paul had established the church in Thessalonica, perhaps about AD 50. Only Galatians may be earlier. They may, in fact, be the earliest writings preserved in the New Testament.

B. They are eschatological, in that they deal with the second coming.

1. The first letter apparently answers two questions:

- What will happen to the dead in Christ when He returns? The answer: They will be raised first (1 Thess 4:13–18).
- When will Christ return? The answer: No one knows; He will come like a thief; but be prepared (1 Thess 5:1–6).

2. The second letter deals with misunderstandings regarding the second coming.

- Apparently, some were teaching errors regarding the subject, perhaps even claiming to represent Paul in doing so (2 Thess 2:1, 2). They apparently believed that Christ had already returned.
- Others apparently were convinced that Christ's coming would be immediate. Paul taught them that something else had to happen first—the man of lawlessness had first to be revealed (2 Thess 2:1–11).
- This doctrinal understanding may have caused them to make a practical mistake—to quit working while they waited for the Lord's return. Paul said that they had to work (2 Thess 3:6–15). (But this was also a problem Paul addressed in his first letter; see 1 Thess 4:11).

C. They are written to a very good church. Paul is as complimentary to this church as he is to any other. See especially 1 Thessalonians 1:2–8. See also: 1 Thessalonians 2:13; 3:6, 7; 4:10. See also 2 Corinthians 8:1–5.

D. The church at Thessalonica was experiencing persecution.

- Perhaps persecution should have been expected. See Acts 17:5–9.
- Notice: 1 Thessalonians 1:6; 2:14; 3:3–5; 2 Thessalonians 1:4–10.

THE CITY OF THESSALONICA

A. In Macedonia, which was the northern province of Greece.

B. The capital city of Macedonia.

C. It exists today with the same name, as the second (next to Athens) most important city of Greece.

PAUL'S RELATIONSHIP WITH THE CHURCH AT THESSALONICA

A. On the second missionary journey, after leaving Philippi (Acts 16), and leaving Luke in Philippi, Paul, Silas, and Timothy went on to Thessalonica.

B. The record of their visit is found in Acts 17:1–10. It is hard to understand how all that Paul says about Thessalonica could have happened in only three weeks.

C. From there, Paul and Silas went on to Berea. Timothy may have come later (Acts 17:11–15).

D. Paul then went on to Athens, leaving Silas and Timothy in Berea. Timothy may have come to him there, but

Paul sent him back to Thessalonica (Acts 17:16–33; 1 Thess 3:1, 2).

E. From Athens Paul went to Corinth (Acts 18:1–4). Silas and Timothy joined him (Acts 18:5) and brought help from Macedonia (2 Cor 11:8, 9), which could have included Thessalonica.

F. At this time Timothy reported to Paul concerning Thessalonica. Paul had been anxious to hear; he had even wanted to visit the church there himself (1 Thess 2:18). The news from Thessalonica was good! (1 Thess 3:6–10). At this time apparently, Timothy brought to Paul the questions concerning the second coming.

G. Thus, at this time Paul wrote 1 Thessalonians. Notice 1 Thessalonians 1:1; Corinth was the only place where these three men were together.

H. A few months later further word reached Paul—perhaps the bearer of the first letter (whose name we do not know) brought it—about the church, with the result that he wrote 2 Thessalonians. Thus, the two letters were written within a few months of each other from Corinth by Paul on the second missionary journey, not long after the church in Thessalonica was established. The date would have been not long after 50 (*CMM*, 347; 50–51, House, 16; 50–51, Harrison, 264).

I. It's possible that Paul visited the church again on the third missionary journey. See Acts 20:1, 3.

WHAT PURPOSES DID THESE EPISTLES SERVE?

What message(s) did Paul have for the church in Thessalonica? They were written:

A. To express Paul's love and concern for the church (1 Thess 2:7–11; 2:17–3:13; 2 Thess 1:3, 4).

B. To urge the church to press on, to "more and more" do the will of the Lord.

- Of whom did this church consist? See Acts 17:4. Yet apparently, the majority of the church was made up of former idol worshipers (1 Thess 1:9).
- But the church had become marvelously faithful. See references above.
- What do you say to a church that is already faithful? Do "more and more" (1 Thess 4:1, 10).
- Apparently, they did exactly that (See 2 Thess 1:3).

C. To answer questions about the second coming. See above.

D. To help the church in a time of persecution. What sort of help was provided?

- It would help them to remember that Paul was persecuted (1 Thess 2:2).
- ...and to remember that other churches had been persecuted (1 Thess 2:14).
- ...and that Christ had been persecuted (1 Thess 2:15).
- ...and that their persecutors would themselves be punished (2 Thess 1:6–9; 1 Thess 2:16).
- ...and that the afflictions had been predicted (1 Thess 3:4).

- In light of their persecutions what they needed was faith, or faithfulness (1 Thess 3:7–10; 2 Thess 1:4; 2:14).
- Faith would issue in righteous living (1 Thess 5:23; 2 Thess 1:11).
- The Lord would help (2 Thess 3:3).
- Paul had confidence in them (2 Thess 3:4).

E. To respond to false teachers and teachings.

- Paul's emphasis on his own work and methods and concern—1 Thessalonians 2:1–13—may suggest that he had detractors among the Thessalonians (or who had come into the church since he left).
- 2 Thessalonians 2:2 specifically mentions that false teaching concerning the second coming was circulating, perhaps even in Paul's name.

F. To deal with a particular problem: What do you do about people who will not work?

- The problem may have existed already when Paul wrote 1 Thessalonians. See 1 Thessalonians 2:9 and 4:10, 11.
- But it had apparently become a greater problem when Paul wrote 2 Thessalonians (2 Thess 3:6–15).
- What should be done? Withdraw from such a one!

G. To provide practical instructions regarding the Christian life. See especially 1 Thessalonians 4:1–8; 5:12–22.

HOW CAN WE DIFFERENTIATE BETWEEN THESE TWO EPISTLES?

A. Both are about the second coming, but they answer different questions about that coming:

- First: (a) What will happen to the dead in Christ when He returns? (b) When will He return?
- Second: Will His coming be immediate, or must something else happen first?

B. In both, the church is commended, but there is more of a personal nature, more about the relationship between Paul and the church, and more commendation, in the first letter.

C. Perhaps the best way to distinguish between them is to remember:

- The first is about a young church which is highly commended, and told to continue what it is doing, only to do it "more and more."
- The second deals with specific problems: Will the Lord's coming be immediate? And what do you do about Christians who will not work?

CRITICAL ISSUE

Is 2 Thessalonians really by the apostle Paul? "II Thessalonians is the least questioned of Paul's letters. The order from least to most questioned of Paul's letters is II Thessalonians, Colossians, Ephesians, Pastorals" (Black, 10).

A. The main reason to reject it is a delayed eschatology (2 Thess 2), which is thought to be atypical for Paul. But this is probably misreading Paul and misunderstanding what the New Testament elsewhere teaches.

B. Arguments for authenticity (from Black, 11):

- Polycarp and Marcion treat the letter as Pauline.
- The style and vocabulary are Pauline.
- Paul is concerned about certifying his authorship (2 Thess 3:17).

Notes on the Pastoral Epistles

CLASSIFYING THESE EPISTLES

A. THE THREE EPISTLES DISCUSSED ARE I TIMOTHY, 2 Timothy, and Titus.

B. They are called "pastoral" because they are written to preachers or evangelists, who are usually thought to be "pastors." It needs to be remembered that, in the New Testament, "pastors" are "elders," and a preacher is not a "pastor" just because he is a preacher—though he may do "pastoring" or "shepherding" kinds of things.

C. The epistles do deal with *elders*, who are also called *pastors*, giving their qualifications. Likewise, they deal with church government, which involves the appointment and work of pastors, or elders. In this sense, the epistles' designation is appropriate.

D. Other classifications:

- Hiebert classifies their content as being *ecclesiological* (about the Church of Christ), and suggests that they are about the organization of the church.
- Tenney's (*New Testament Survey*) chapter on these letters is titled: "The Institutional Church: The Pastoral Epistles."
- It has been suggested that they might be called the "Organizational Epistles."
- They have been taught in a preacher training school under the title "Evangelistic Epistles," because they deal with the work of the evangelist, or preacher.

CRITICAL ISSUE: WERE THESE EPISTLES WRITTEN BY PAUL IN THE FIRST CENTURY?

"Contemporary critical orthodoxy insists that the Pastorals were all written by someone other than Paul and at a time considerably later than that of the apostle" (*CMM*, 360).

A. There is agreement that the three documents "be treated as a unit" with regard to authorship (Harrison, 351).

B. According to Harrison (351), three positions have been taken:

1. The traditional viewpoint: Paul wrote them near the end of his life. Variations include the following (Black, 23):

- Paul dictated the letters.
- Paul allowed his amanuensis (secretary) a great deal of freedom.

2. The fragment theory: They contain fragments written by Paul, but these are included by a later writer along with his own material.

3. The fictional (pseudonymous) approach: They are the work of a Paulinist "who took the liberty of writing in Paul's name to avail himself of the prestige and authority of the apostle in order to counteract the evils of the day and strengthen the Christian community." In this case, they are dated to the early part of the second century.

C. Evidence:

1. External evidence. There is little or no reason to reject Paul's authorship of these books in the external evidence. Although, according to Black, "the tradition favoring Paul as the author is weaker than for the rest of the Pauline literature," the case against Paul in the tradition is not particularly strong (25).

2. Internal evidence. It is on the basis of the internal evidence that many reject Paul as the author.

a. Evidence for Paul's authorship: The ascription of the books to Paul. It is alleged that using another's name would not have been regarded as a forgery or as deceit, but this cannot be proved and is in fact unlikely.

b. Evidence against Paul's authorship with answers given.

(1) Historical data in the pastorals "cannot be fitted into Paul's known life and labors prior to the journey to Rome" (Harrison, 354). This cannot be acknowledged but can be explained by the supposition that Paul was released after his first imprisonment in Rome. In favor of a second imprisonment (Black, 24):

- "In Acts Paul is innocent and probably would be released." The prison epistles all seem to indicate that Paul expected to be released. In 2 Timothy Paul is about to die.
- Clement (1 Clement 5:7) says that Paul went to the "limit of the west," which probably suggests Spain, thus implying a release from Paul's first imprisonment. Other early writings also indicate that Paul was released from prison.

(2) "The organizational emphasis is said to be contrary to Paul and later than his time" (Harrison, 356). But Paul in other places showed concern about elders. Furthermore, these books do not presuppose the existence of a monarchal bishop and so do not have to have come from a time later than the first century (Harrison, 357).

(3) Style and language of the epistles. "No doubt there is considerable difference between these epistles and the other Paulines" (Harrison, 358).

- But the differences may be explained by: (i) different occasions and different purposes, (ii) differences in Paul—here may be a more mature Paul at a different stage of his life, (iii) possibly the use of a different secretary (Harrison, 363; citing Moule, he notes, 365, that the amanuensis may have been Luke), (iv) Paul's not using an amanuensis (Black, 223).
- Also, there are similarities between these letters and other writings of Paul.

(4) "The doctrinal outlook and emphasis is said to be different from that of Paul" (Harrison, 360). But there are certain assumptions at work here: A scholar assumes that Paul's major writings (Romans, 1 and 2 Corinthians, and Galatians) reflect Paul's theology, and then judges any other writings by these letters. If the other letters do not reflect the same emphasis, then they must not have been written by Paul. This obviously ignores both the fact that Paul would have had other purposes in writing other letters, and the obvious truth that to understand Paul's theology one needs to consider all that Paul wrote—not just the few epistles he thinks are most impressive. Harrison says, "The argument ... is weakened by the fact that the Pastorals are practical to an uncommon degree and are therefore less theological" (361).

(5) It is objected that the writer "makes Paul treat Timothy as a mere youth and liable to be despised on that account (I Tim. 4:12)" (Harrison, 362). But men were considered "young" until they were forty years old; thus the danger suggested in 1 Timothy 4:12, assuming that others were older, was real. See Harrison, 362.

c. Evidence against pseudonymity.

(1) There is evidence that Paul was concerned that others did not write in his name (2 Thess 2:2; 3:17). There is other evidence in the New Testament to indicate that the writers were concerned that their works be accepted as genuine, indicating that the early church was inclined to reject some works as inauthentic.

(2) There is evidence from early writings that the practice of plagiarism was unacceptable. In particular, pseudonymous letters among early Christians were rare or nonexistent. (CMM, 367, 368.)

(3) The following facts regarding the determination of the canon argue against the widespread acceptance of pseudonymity:

- the question of authorship dominated the question of what books to accept as inspired,
- obviously, pseudonymous works were rejected, and
- anonymous writings were more likely to be questioned.

(4) If there was one pseudonymous writer, why did he write three books? And why did he invent trips and visits and other details that Acts does not mention?

DATE OF THE EPISTLES

A. They are the last of the epistles written by Paul.

B. They were written in this order: 1 Timothy, Titus, 2 Timothy.

C. In 2 Timothy Paul was a prisoner, but not, apparently, in the other two letters. 2 Timothy could, therefore, be thought of as a "prison epistle."

D. The travels, places, situations, and people mentioned in these letters do *not* fit into any of Paul's travels in Acts. Therefore, all were written *after* Acts—or after the events recorded in Acts. Paul was released after that first imprisonment in Rome, conducted further missionary work, perhaps traveled to Spain, was imprisoned again (the second imprisonment), and finally died in Rome.

1. 1 Timothy and Titus were written after the first imprisonment and before the second imprisonment. Dates:

- 1 Timothy—early fall of the year AD 63 from Macedonia.
- Titus—from Corinth, during the fall of AD 63, after Paul's arrival there from Crete.

2. Second Timothy was written from Rome during the second imprisonment in the early autumn of AD 66 just before Paul's death. (According to Hiebert, who assigns the first two to Paul's works *before* his journey to Spain, and the last to Paul's imprisonment *after* that journey.)

A RECONSTRUCTION OF PAUL'S LIFE AFTER HIS FIRST IMPRISONMENT, FROM THE PASTORAL EPISTLES

(From Hiebert, 322, 323. For another viewpoint, see the introduction to the epistles in the Harper Study Bible.)

1. The release at Rome. This apparently occurred in the late spring of AD 63 and was in accordance with the hope expressed in the Prison Epistles (Phlm 22; Phil 2:23, 24).
2. The sending of Timothy to Philippi. As soon as the outcome of the trial was announced, Paul dispatched Timothy to Philippi as he had promised (Phil 2:19–23). Timothy probably took the land route, going along the Appian and the Egnatian Ways, to Philippi, stopping at

Thessalonica with the news of Paul's release. He was apparently instructed to meet Paul at Ephesus.

3. The journey to Asia. Probably Paul went directly to provincial Asia by sea. Arriving at Ephesus, Paul made a short visit there and then went on Colossae, according to his promise to Philemon (Phlm 22), and to the neighboring churches in the Lycus Valley.

4. The return to Ephesus. At Ephesus Paul encountered some heretical teachers and found it necessary to attend to the expulsion of Hymanaeus and Alexander (1 Tim 1:20). Timothy rejoined Paul at Ephesus. The situation in Asia apparently convinced Paul of the necessity of leaving Timothy there to repel the further development of the errors (1 Tim 1:3, 4).

5. The journey into Macedonia. Leaving Timothy to supervise the work at Ephesus, Paul left for Macedonia (1 Tim 1:3). He had hoped to return to Ephesus before long but conditions might detain him for some time, so he wrote I Timothy from Macedonia (1 Tim 3:14, 15).

6. The visit to Crete. Apparently, Paul was able to return to Ephesus as he had planned. From Ephesus, Paul went to Crete where apparently Titus was already at work. Because Paul could not stay there very long to continue with the work, he left Titus there to complete the organization of the churches and to repel the errorists in Crete.

7. Journey to Corinth. From Crete, Paul went on to visit the believers at Corinth. Here he came into touch with Zenas and Apollos who were planning a journey that would take them by Crete. Taking the opportunity thus afforded him, Paul wrote the Letter to Titus and sent it with them. In this letter he announced his plans to winter at Nicopolis and asked Titus to join him there when a replacement worker had been sent to Crete (3:12). The selection of Nicopolis reveals that Paul was planning a trip to the West in the spring.

8. In the spring of AD 64, Paul left Nicopolis for work in Spain. He remained there for perhaps two years. Thus, Paul was away in Spain at the time of the burning of Rome (July 19–24, AD 64) and the beginning of the consequent persecution of the Christians, which Zahn thinks began in October of that year.

9. The return to the East. If Paul remained in Spain for two years, he would be returning to the East as soon as navigation opened up in the spring of AD 66. He would most likely avoid Rome and go directly to the East. Hints of some of the places visited on the journey are found in 2 Timothy. Mention is made of a visit at Troas with Carpus, with whom he left his cloak and his books and parchments (4:13). He found it necessary to leave his companion Trophimus at Miletus because of sickness (4:20). He seems

also to have been at Corinth where Erastus remained (4:20).

10. The imprisonment in Rome. 2 Timothy reveals that Paul again became a prisoner. Where and when Paul was again taken into imprisonment is not revealed. Lewin contends that the fact that Paul left his books and parchments at Troas, materials vitally necessary for his missionary labors, shows that he was arrested at Troas. Back East once more, his many enemies soon contrived to bring about Paul's arrest as a leader of the Christian sect, now officially branded as an illegal religion.

THE RECIPIENTS OF THE LETTERS

A. Where were they when they received the letters?

- Timothy was in Ephesus when Paul wrote I Timothy (1:3).
- Titus was in Crete when Paul wrote to him (1:5).
- It is not definitely known where Timothy was when Paul wrote 2 Timothy. Probably he was in Ephesus (1:18; 4:12).

B. Who were they?

1. They were evangelists, or preachers (1 Tim 4:6; 6:11; 2 Tim 2:2; 4:5; see also other references, as, e.g., 2 Cor 8:23), *not* pastors.

2. They are usually thought to be young (1 Tim 4:12).

Timothy could not have been very young. The Bible does not say that Titus was young.

3. They were Paul's associates, fellow workers, representatives, or helpers.

4. They were both Paul's converts (Titus 1:4; 1 Tim 1:2).

5. Specifically, concerning Timothy:

- A resident of Lystra (Acts 16:1–3).
- Father a Greek, mother a Jewess (Acts 16:2, 3). Paul had him circumcised.
- Mother was Eunice, grandmother was Lois (2 Tim 1:5).
- Names means "honored by God" or "honoring God."
- Raised to know the scriptures (2 Tim 1:5; 3:15).
- Paul's convert. (On the first missionary journey?)
- Circumcised by Paul (Acts 16:4).
- Ordained by the elders and by Paul (1 Tim 4:14; 2 Tim 1:6).
- A constant companion of Paul (Acts 17:14; 18:5; 19:22; 20:3, 4; 1 Cor 4:14; 16:10–12; 2 Cor 1:1; Phil 2:19, 23, 24; 1 Thess 1:1; 3:1, 2; 2 Thess 1:1; Phlm 22).
- He went with Paul on the second missionary journey, was with Paul on the third journey in Ephesus (Acts 19:22), and accompanied Paul on the journey back to Jerusalem (Acts 20:4).
- Paul held Timothy in the highest regard (Phil 2:20–22). Speculations concerning his weaknesses and timidity are based on insufficient evidence.

- He was afflicted with a physical problem (1 Tim 5:23).
- Paul wanted Timothy with him at the end (2 Tim 4:9).

6. Concerning Titus:

- Not mentioned in Acts.
- Was a Greek (Gal 2:3).
- Paul would not let him be circumcised as a kind of "test case."
- Worked with the church in Corinth (2 Cor 8:6, 10).
- Worked with the church in Crete (Titus).
- Had been with Paul during his second imprisonment, but at the time Paul wrote 2 Timothy had gone to Dalmatia (2 Tim 4:10).
- Paul calls him his son in the faith (Titus 1:4), his brother (2 Cor 2:13), and his partner and fellow worker (2 Cor 8:23).
- It is usually thought that Titus was extremely able, especially capable of dealing with difficult situations, and older than Timothy.

THE MESSAGE OF THESE EPISTLES

A. They are about church leadership.

1. Qualifications are given for elders and deacons in 1 Timothy 3 and for elders in Titus 1. *Elders, pastors, and bishops* are three words that apply to the same office or work.

2. The preacher's work is described:

- To live right (1 Tim 4:12, et al.).
- To preach and teach authoritatively (1 Tim 4:1–5, et al.).
- To "set the church in order"—that is, to see that church leaders are properly appointed, false teachers are defeated, etc.
- To train other men like himself (2 Tim 2:2).

B. They are about the church and how people ought to act in it.

- Like Philemon, they are addressed to individuals.
- But unlike Philemon, they are mainly about church organization and doctrine and instructions to preachers. Though written to individuals, they were intended to be read by and to benefit churches.
- See 1 Timothy 3:14, 15: "... I am writing these instructions to you so that ... you may know how one ought to behave in the household of God, which is the church of the living God ..."

C. They are about false teachers and teachings.

Remember Paul's warning in Acts 20 to the elders at Ephesus. The false teachings mentioned and listed below were not necessarily common to the situation reflected in all three letters.

- "Myths and endless genealogies" (1 Tim 1:4).
- False ideas about the law (1 Tim 1:7ff).

- False ideas which led to immorality (?) (1 Tim 1:9–11).
- Rejecting conscience (1 Tim 1:19, 20).
- Profiting from their teachings, greedy (1 Tim 6:3–5).
- Held that the resurrection was already past (2 Tim 2:18).
- In Crete, there were some of the circumcision party (Titus 1:10). They taught Jewish myths (Titus 1:14).
- False teaching may have led to evil deeds (Titus 1:16).

D. They predict a coming apostasy (1 Tim 4:1ff; 2 Tim 3:1ff; 2 Tim 4:1ff).

E. They provide practical instructions for all groups.

This was "sound (healthy) doctrine." For example, see Titus 2.

HOW CAN THESE EPISTLES BE DIFFERENTIATED?

A. "In I Timothy the emphasis is more on sound doctrine; in Titus, on worthy conduct." (Hiebert, 346.)

B. Tenney identifies them like this:

- 1 Timothy: Advice to a young preacher.
- Titus: The sound doctrine.
- 2 Timothy: The farewell message.

C. Black (25, 26) identifies the following purposes for these letters:

- 1 Timothy — To help Timothy control false teachers at Ephesus.
- Titus — To help Titus oppose false teaching at Crete and to encourage behavior that is appealing to outsiders.
- 2 Timothy — To encourage Timothy to persevere, to summon him to Paul's side in Rome, and to encourage him to teach against false teaching.

Notes on Philemon

INTRODUCTION

A. Philemon is one of the prison epistles (Phlm 1, 12, 13).

B. It is one of four one-chapter books in the New Testament. The other three are 2 and 3 John and Jude.

C. It was apparently carried by Onesimus and Tychicus, along with the letters to Colossians and Ephesians (Eph 6:21; Col 4:7).

D. Generally, the same people are mentioned as being with Paul in Colossians and Philemon.

E. Philemon was written by Paul (Phlm 1:1), who associates Timothy with him in his salutation, just as he does in Colossians and Philippians. Paul's authorship is undisputed.

F. It was written to Philemon (1:1), as well as to Apphia and Archippus and to the church which met in their house.

G. "Onesimus is identified elsewhere as coming from

Colossae (Col 4:9), as is Archippus who is mentioned in the opening greeting of this letter (v. 2; Col 4:17). Hence Philemon and the church in his house were in Colossae" (*The New Oxford Annotated Bible*, NASV).

H. It is a personal letter about a personal matter, but it was still to be read by the church.

CONTEXT, PURPOSE

A. Philemon was a good man: Paul's friend and co-worker, whose house served as the meeting place for a congregation (1, 2); whose love and faith were well known (4, 5); who had refreshed the hearts of the saints (7); who would be very willing to prepare a guest room for Paul (22).

B. The story that lies behind the letter can be reconstructed as follows:

1. Onesimus, whose name means "useful" or "beneficial," was Philemon's slave, but had apparently run away from Philemon. He may have stolen something in doing so (18, 19).

2. He had gone to wherever Paul was (Rome?) and there Paul had converted him (10).

3. Now Paul was sending him back to Philemon (12).

4. The primary purpose of the letter was to persuade Philemon to receive Onesimus back as a brother (16, 17).

5. Paul apparently had another purpose as well: He wanted Philemon to send Onesimus back to him so that he might help Paul in Paul's work (1:11–14. See also 21).

CONTRIBUTION

A. This book contributes to the discussion of slavery as it affected Christians in the first century.

B. It also shows us Paul at his most persuasive. How did Paul go about persuading Philemon to do what he suggested?

1. He complimented Philemon (4–7).

2. He appealed to Philemon on the basis of who and what he (Paul) was—one who had the right to command but chose to appeal (8, 9), an old man (9), a prisoner of Christ, Philemon's own partner (17).

3. He appealed to Philemon on the basis of his (Paul's) relationship with and love for Onesimus (10, 12, 13, 16, 17).

4. He appealed to Philemon on the basis of Philemon's best interests: Onesimus was now "profitable" (NRSV: "useful") to him (11).

5. He appealed to Philemon on the basis of Philemon's relationship to Onesimus—formerly useless, now useful (11); one who could serve in Philemon's place (13); a relationship temporarily severed, but now forever established (15); formerly a slave, now a beloved brother and again a member of Philemon's household (16).

6. He appealed to Philemon on the basis of Philemon's concern for the work of Christ (13, 14).

7. He appealed to Philemon's sense of duty. Even his saying that he wanted Philemon's action to be voluntary and not forced (14) would have appealed to Philemon's sense of "oughtness"—his desire to "do the right thing" (See also 8, 21).

8. He appealed to Philemon's sense of gratitude, for what he had done for Philemon (17–19).

9. He appealed to Philemon on the basis of his own relationship with Philemon (See v. 20, et al.).

10. He expressed confidence that Philemon would indeed do what he should (v 21).

C. It also contributes to our appreciation of how the gospel could break down social, economic, and ethnic barriers in the first century. Philemon, a (possibly) wealthy Greek or Roman; Paul, a zealous Jew; and Onesimus, a lowly slave—all were to be brothers loved by one another.

Notes on Hebrews

THE BOOK OF HEBREWS IS DIFFERENT

AS EVIDENCED BY THE BEGINNING:

A. It does not name the author.

B. It does not name the recipient.

C. The writer calls it a "word of exhortation" (Heb 13:22).

D. Someone said that it begins like a sermon, continues like an essay, and concludes like a letter. It may have been something like a sermon, or sermons (which were put together), to which was added the epistolary closing so that it it could be sent to a particular church.

THIS ALMOST CERTAINLY LED TO SOME HESITANCE IN INCLUDING HEBREWS IN THE CANON OF THE NEW TESTAMENT.

The following is from Carson, Moo, and Morris, *An Introduction to the New Testament*, 404.

A. The question of canonicity was tied to the question of authorship.

B. It was always accepted in the Eastern church, in part because it was thought to have come from Paul. One of the earliest of the papyri (P46), which dates to the early third century, includes it in a collection of Paul's letters.

C. It was "widely known and quoted" in the Western church, but "it was not at first received as canonical." The Muratorian Canon excludes it. Eusebius put it among the "acknowledged," books, "though he is aware of doubts in the West."

D. According to *CMM*, the influence of Jerome and Augustine ultimately led to the acceptance of Hebrews by the Western church.

THIS DIFFERENCE ALSO LED TO QUESTIONS ABOUT AUTHORSHIP.

For information about the various possibilities concerning authorship, see House, 140–144.

A. Paul is sometimes thought to be the author of the book.

- The end of it sounds like Paul.
- There is a tradition that Paul wrote it.

- Many of the ideas found in it are similar to the ideas of Paul.
- Very few would today defend Paul's authorship.

B. But Paul's authorship is generally rejected by scholars today.

- There is no good explanation as to why Paul would leave off his name.
- The style is different. "The Greek of Hebrews is more polished than that of Paul, and the consistent quality of the rhetoric quite remarkable" (*CMM*, 395).
- The theology is not typical of Paul.
- It is highly unlikely that Paul would have used the words found in Hebrews 2:3 — "attested to us by those who heard him."

C. Others have been suggested as the author:

- Apollos. Described as "a native of Alexandria . . . an eloquent man, well-versed in the scriptures" (Acts 18:24), he was the kind of man who might write such a book.
- Barnabas. A Levite, who was named by the apostles "Son of Encouragement" (or "exhortation") (Acts 4:36). He might have written such a "word of exhortation" (Heb 13:22).
- Luke. A well-educated Gentile, who would have been familiar with the Septuagint and capable of

writing good Greek. He might have written a book in the good Greek style in which Hebrews is written. There are some similarities between the Greek of Luke-Acts and the Greek of Hebrews. (One theory, dating from the second century, has Paul as the author and Luke as the person who translated Paul's Hebrew letter or wrote down Paul's thoughts (*CMM*, 395).

- Priscilla and Aquila. Since they were Jews and were capable of instructing Apollos (Acts 18:26ff), this wife-and-husband team would have been capable of writing Hebrews. Since Priscilla was the leading member of the pair, the fact that she was a woman explains why there is no identification of the author at the beginning of the book. However, the participle translated "to tell" in Hebrews 11:32, which has as its antecedent "me" (the author) is singular and masculine, suggesting a male, rather than a female, author.

D. The conclusion? No one knows for sure. Origen believed that the book came from Paul but was written down by one of his disciples; he wrote, "But who wrote the epistle, in truth God knows" (*CMM*, 395).

E. Some things may be deduced about the author from the book itself. See *CMM*, 397.

IT HAS ALSO LED TO QUESTIONS ABOUT WHO RECEIVED IT.

A. It says "to the Hebrews." But this is not inspired. It is a deduction from the subject matter. Since the book deals with Jewish subjects, contrasts the Old Law with the New, and refers to the Old Testament constantly, it is thought that the first readers were Jewish Christians. But this is not certain.

- The description of the Old Covenant requires only "book knowledge." To understand the message, one would not have to have experienced first-century Judaism.
- Gentile Christians would have been well acquainted with the Old Testament.

B. Various opinions have been advanced as to where they lived. Hebrews 13:24 says, "Those from Italy send you greetings." But this doesn't solve the problem. The writer may or may not have been in Italy and may or may not have been writing to Italy.

1. Two places in particular have gained support:

- Palestine, especially Jerusalem. But how then can the absence of references to the temple be explained? Why is the book in Greek and why does it depend exclusively on the Septuagint?
- Rome. This fits Hebrew 13:24 well; Rome was the first place where the epistle was known; and the contents of the letter can be explained in terms of its being addressed to a house church in

Rome. But there is no proof; Rome is just a guess.

C. Do we know any more about these Christians?

1. They were known by the author, and he knew them well (Heb 13:22–25).

2. They had been Christians for some time (Heb 5:12ff).

3. They had experienced persecution and expected to experience more of it (Heb 10:32–34; 12:3–11).

4. They were in danger of falling away. See the passages below. What was the nature of this apostasy?

- There was a doctrinal aspect to their apostasy; they were in danger of being led away by false teachings (13:7–10); usually it is thought that the recipients were Jewish Christians who had left Judaism but were in danger of again embracing the Law of Moses and of going back into Judaism.

- There was also a practical element to the apostasy: They were in danger of becoming "sluggish" about their faith (6:12); apparently they were dispirited and apathetic and lethargic; the writer admonishes them to "lift your drooping hands and strengthen your weak knees" (12:12); they had not grown as they should (5:11–14ff); and they needed to be exhorted not to neglect to meet together, "as is the habit of some" (10:25).

THERE IS ALSO NO AGREEMENT ABOUT ITS DATE.

A. Since we don't know for sure who wrote the book or to whom, it is very difficult to date Hebrews.

B. A lower limit is suggested by Hebrews 2:2, 3: the writer classifies himself and his readers together as being "second generation" Christians. An upper limit is suggested by the mention of Timothy in 13:23 and by the use of Hebrews by Clement about AD 96.

C. The persecution mentioned in the book proves little since isolated persecutions broke out in every decade after the establishment of the church.

D. The only other datum that counts for much is the absence of any mention of the temple and of its destruction in AD 70. If the temple had been destroyed, and thus the sacrificial system had been stopped, surely the writer would have mentioned it.

E. It seems likely, therefore, that the letter to the Hebrews was written before AD 70. (See the discussion in *CMM*, 398–400)

WHAT IS HEBREWS ABOUT?

A. Its purpose: to keep the readers from apostasy! They were in danger of:

- "Drifting away" from the truth (2:1).
- Having an "evil, unbelieving heart that turns away from the living God" (3:13).

- Falling by disobedience as did the Israelites (4:11).
- Committing apostasy to the point that they will be unable to repent (6:4–6).
- Becoming like worthless ground fit for nothing but to be cursed (6:7, 8).
- Persisting in sin to the extent that "there no longer remains a sacrifice for sins, but a fearful prospect of judgment" (10:26, 27ff).
- Abandoning their confidence (10:35).
- Shrinking back and being lost (10:39).
- Failing "to obtain the grace of God" (12:15ff).
- Rejecting the message they had received from heaven (12:25).

B. Its theme: Better! Everything about Christ is better than everything about the Old Covenant. See the following passages:

- Christ is a better spokesman (1:1, 2).
- Christ is greater than the angels (1:4).
- He is worthy of more glory than Moses (3:3)
- His priesthood is better than the Levitical priesthood (7:7, 15, 23–28, et al.).
- We have a better hope (7:19).
- We have a better covenant (7:22; 8:6).
- Christ has a more excellent ministry. (A better priesthood?) (8:6).
- We have better promises (8:6).
- We have a better sacrifice (9:9, 10, 12–14, 23; 10:1–4, 10–18).

- Christ ministers from a better sanctuary (9:11, 23, 24; 12:18–24).
- We possess "something better and more lasting" (10:34).
- The patriarchs looked for a "better country" (11:16).
- Some anticipated a "better resurrection" (11:35).
- Something better had been provided for us (11:40).
- Christ's blood speaks a "better word" than that of Abel (12:24).

C. Its (primary) subject: The priesthood (8:1). To this subject can be connected the emphasis on a better sacrifice and a better sanctuary.

Notes on the General Epistles

THE BOOKS IN THIS CATEGORY

- Always included in this category are: James, 1 and 2 Peter, 1 and 2 and 3 John, and Jude.
- House includes Hebrews in this category (*Chronological and Background Charts of the New Testament*, 19), but we will not consider the book of Hebrews under this heading.

THE MEANING OF THE DESIGNATION "GENERAL"

A. The first use of the term:

Eusebius is the first to apply the term "catholic epistles" (ca. 324) to a collection of letters: James, Jude, 2 Peter, and 2 and 3 John, which he also designated as "disputed letters," i.e., not having universal acceptance in the church. As the process of formation of a New Testament canon drew to a close, 1 Peter and 1 John were added to the Catholic Epistle corpus as evidenced by Athanasius's so-called Festal Letter of 367 (Hebrews is designated a Pauline work). "General Letters," *Mercer Dictionary of the Bible*, 320.

B. The idea of "general" or "catholic" seems to be that they were written to the brotherhood generally, rather than to a specific church, as for instance the letters of Paul to the churches at Corinth or Philippi.

C. This, however, does not really distinguish these books.

- Some of the books were indeed written to groups of churches (though not necessarily to the brotherhood as a whole)—see James and 1 and (possibly) 2 Peter. But consider that Galatians was also written to a group of churches.
- Other of the "general epistles" were written to individuals—see 2 and 3 John—just as Paul's letters to Timothy, Titus, and Philemon were written to individuals.
- Only 1 John and Jude say or imply virtually nothing about the Christians to whom they are writing.

D. Perhaps the main thing that distinguishes these books is that they were not written by Paul.

E. The fact that they are found together in our New

Testament gives evidence that they have been considered to have something in common.

THE MAIN CRITICAL ISSUE REGARDING THE GENERAL EPISTLES

A. The most important critical issue regarding these books has to do with their acceptance into the canon.

B. Thus, of these books:

- 1 John and 1 Peter were the most quickly accepted.
- The others were placed by Eusebius in a category he called "disputed letters." (See above.)

C. Eventually, however, all were accepted in the canon. "The inclusion in the canon of the General Letters ... is a forceful statement of the conviction of the early church that these works are an authentic, authoritative expression of Christian faith" (*MDB*, 321).

A. Are there reasons why some of these books would not have been readily accepted? The reasons vary, but some possibilities are:

- The indefiniteness of address. See Harrison, 120.
- The shortness of the books.
- Uncertainty about the author.

THE THEMES OF THE GENERAL EPISTLES

Some possibilities:

- James — Practical Christianity
- 1 Peter — Coping with Persecution
- 2 Peter — Facing False Teaching
- 1 John — Assurance
- 2 John — Rejecting False Teachers
- 3 John — Receiving Christ's Messengers
- Jude — Contend for the Faith

Notes on James

AUTHOR

A. The book claims to have been written by "James, a servant of God and of the Lord Jesus Christ" (Jas 1:1).

B. There are four men called James who are spoken of in the New Testament:

1. James the apostle, the son of Zebedee, brother of John. See Mark 1:19; 5:37; 9:2; 10:35; 14:33.
2. James the son of Alphaeus, also an apostle (Mark 3:18; Acts 1:13). (Maybe this was "James the younger" in Mark 15:40. Carson, Moo, and Morris, 410.)
3. James the father (or brother) of Judas the apostle (Acts 1:13; see also John 14:22). (Judas the apostle is also called Thaddaeus in Mark 3:18 and Matt 10:3).

4. James the Lord's brother, who was a well-known leader in the church in Jerusalem (Mark 6:3; Gal 1:19; 2:9; Acts 12:17; 15:13; 21:18).

C. Of these four, James the son of Alphaeus, and James the father of Judas can probably be eliminated as not being sufficiently well known to have written such a letter with the expectation that it would be accepted.

D. Probably James the apostle was put to death too early (ca. AD 44—see Acts 12:2) to be the author of the epistle (*CMM*, 410).

E. Thus, it is likely that James the Lord's brother, who was a leader in the church in Jerusalem, is the author.

1. In favor of this viewpoint:

a. There is a weak tradition that the brother of Jesus wrote the epistle.

b. Internal evidence is consistent with this theory (*CMM*, 410).

- The authority with which the writer speaks.
- The allusions to the teachings of Jesus.
- The "Jewishness" of the book.
- The similarity between the language of the book and the speech given by James in Acts 15. (See, for example, Harrison, 387, 388.)

2. Against:

- The author does not identify himself as a brother of Jesus.

- The Greek of the book is too good for it to have been written by a Palestinian Jew.
- The author's view of faith and works was written to refute Paul's viewpoint, but it reflects a mistaken view of Paul's theology. Therefore, it must have been written much later than Paul.

3. If the author was James the brother of Jesus, what do we know about him?

- A brother of Jesus (probably the oldest) (Mark 6:3; Matt. 13:55).
- Along with his brothers, did not at first believe in Jesus (John 7:2–5).
- Usually assumed that when Jesus died, his brothers were still unbelievers (and that Joseph was dead); otherwise, it would not have been necessary to entrust his mother's keeping to John the apostle (John 19:26, 27).
- Recipient of a special resurrection appearance of the Lord (1 Cor 15:7).
- After the resurrection, the brothers were believers (Acts 1:14).
- A leader of the church in Jerusalem (Gal. 1:19; 2:9, 12; Jude 1; Acts 12:17; 15:13; 21:18).
- According to Josephus, James was put to death in AD 62.
- There are many legends about James, including a tradition that the Jews gave him the name "James the Just."

DATE

A. One's decision regarding the writer will influence the date assigned to the book.

- If James the apostle wrote the book, then it must have been written very early, before ca. 44.
- James, the brother of the Lord, died ca. 62. If he is the author, the book must have been written before that.
- If another James is the author, then it could have been written later.

B. One's view of the purpose of the book will also affect decisions made concerning its date.

- If it was written to correct a misunderstanding of Paul's theology, then it would have probably been written later rather than earlier since it would take some time for Paul's writings to become known.
- *CMM* (414) argues for a date before James was personally acquainted with Paul and his writings, but after Paul had been preaching and teaching for some time—thus, about AD 49. (According to this theory, James knew and refuted only a garbled, mistaken view of Paul's theology.)
- House dates the book in the 40s or 50s (16).

RECIPIENTS

A. The letter is addressed to "the twelve tribes of the dispersion" (1:1).

- "Twelve tribes" speaks of Israel. Though there were no longer twelve tribes, the expression was still used to refer to God's covenant people.
- The people of Israel had been dispersed, beginning with the Assyrian captivity and continuing to the New Testament age. There were Jews living throughout the Roman world.
- Thus, literally, James says that he is writing to the Jews outside of Palestine who are scattered throughout the world.

B. But is this address to be taken literally?
1. Was James writing to Jews who were not Christians?

- The book is indeed very Jewish. E.g., the word "synagogue" is used for "assembly" in James 2:2.
- But this seems unlikely, especially since it was Christians who received and preserved the book.

2. If not, then to whom?
a. According to New Testament writers, Christians composed spiritual Israel. Thus, it seems likely that "the twelve tribes" refers to the church.

b. "Of the dispersion" then may suggest that the Christians addressed were living outside of Palestine.

c. James could have been written to Christians outside of Palestine.

- It is usually thought that these were Jewish Christians (see above). *CMM* connects the addressees with the Jerusalem Christians who were "scattered" (Acts 8:4; 11:19). "Identifying James's readers with these early Jewish Christians would fit the date of the letter and would furnish an explanation of the circumstances that called it forth: James, the leader of the Jerusalem church, must minister to his scattered flock by mail" (*CMM*, 415.).

- The readers may not, however, have been all Jewish Christians. It may be possible to see a parallel in the letter sent out by the "Jerusalem conference" that freed Christians from the law but advised them as to how they ought to live (Acts 15:23–29). The parallel would not be so much in the details of the advice but in the fact that the Jerusalem church felt the need and the right to send it.

MESSAGE

A. The book is hard to outline: "The letter of James, a series of loosely related homilies, resists clear structural demarcation." (*CMM*, 409.) The Introduction to James in the *Harper Study Bible* (RSV) provides the following outline:

- Salutation (1:1)

- True religion (1:2–27)
- True faith (2:1–3:12)
- True wisdom (3:13–5:18)
- Conclusion (5:19, 20).

B. Concerning its message:

- It has much in common with wisdom, or sapiential, literature, such as the Book of Proverbs, since it is "concerned mainly with the practical aspects of the Christian faith, consisting of maxims and counsel for everyday conduct" (*HSB*).
- It has little that is distinctly Christian. The Lord Jesus Christ is mentioned only twice—in 1:1 and 2:1.
- There are strong echoes of the Sermon on the Mount. Thus, though the doctrines about Jesus do not dominate the book, His teachings do.
- James is concerned about the poor and is critical of the rich. See 2:1–8; 5:1–6.

C. Perhaps the outstanding characteristic of the book is that it insists that religion, or faith, must be translated into action. See James 1:22. Its theme could be said to be "Practical Christianity."

D. A controversial aspect of James's teaching is his discussion of the relationship between faith and works, which seems to conflict with Paul's teaching of salvation by faith. Various solutions have been proposed.

1. Two from *CMM* (419):

- "Justify" means different things in Paul and James; in James, it means to "vindicate before people." Works are a demonstration of righteousness.
- "Justify" in James means at the last judgment, whereas in Paul it means initial justification.

2. Another: James and Paul use "faith" and "works" differently. Paul includes "obedience" in faith, James doesn't; Paul uses works in the sense of "meritorious works;" and James uses "works" to refer to "obedience of works."

E. It may be that James wrote the letter to correct a false view of Paul's teaching—a view that Paul knew might exist. If so, then James, like Paul's letters, is also an "occasional" letter—that is, it was written to deal with a particular problem.

OTHER CHARACTERISTICS

- "The flavor of pastoral admonition" (*CMM*, 415). It abounds in imperatives.
- "Extensive and very effective use of metaphors and figures of speech." (*CMM*, 416).
- "The work has an authoritative tone" (Harrison, 383).
- "The epistle is notably impersonal" (Harrison, 384).
- "There is a fine appreciation of nature in this book" (Harrison, 384).

- "The Greek of the epistle is of a high quality ..." (Harrison, 384).

CANONICITY

From *CMM*, 417, 418:

- Apparently influenced several late-first-century works.
- Cited by Origen as scripture, but Origen also noted that it was disputed.
- Eusebius accorded James canonical status but said that it was among the disputed books.
- Earliest clear references to James date from the fourth century.
- Accepted by Jerome.
- Later questioned by Luther because of its theology, but Luther did not drop the book from the canon.

Notes on 1 and 2 Peter

FIRST PETER

A. AUTHOR: THE BOOK CLAIMS TO HAVE BEEN WRITTEN by "Peter, an apostle of Jesus Christ" (1 Pet 1:1).

1. There is good reason to believe that the epistle was written by the apostle Peter.

a. External evidence: Irenaeus is the first to quote it explicitly as a writing of Peter. From that time on it was routinely accepted in the church (Carson, Moo, and Morris, 425).

b. Internal evidence:

(1) The writer's message is consistent with his being an eyewitness and the style is similar to Peter's words in Acts (*CMM*, 421, 422).

(2) Arguments against this viewpoint are not persuasive. They include (from *CMM*, 422, 423):

- The Greek is too good.

- The letter is too dependent on Pauline theology.
- The letter contains "no evidence of a knowledge of the events in Jesus's life."
- The references to persecution make it necessary to believe that the letter was written during the reign of Domitian, which is too late for Peter.

2. What do we know about this Peter? Peter is mentioned by name more than 150 times in the New Testament.

- His name was also Simon; "Peter" means "rock." "The Aramaic equivalent is Cephas" John 1:42; et al. (*Mercer Dictionary of the Bible* 671, 672).
- He was a fisherman, the brother of Andrew, and the son of Jonah (Aramaic; Greek equivalent — John, *MDB*, 672); and he was partners with James and John, the sons of Zebedee. (Matt 4:18; 16:17; Luke 5:10).
- He may have been a disciple of John the Baptist before he became a follower of Christ (John 1:35–42).
- He was one of the first of apostles called by Jesus (Matt 4:18–22).
- He is always listed first in the list of the apostles, thus probably indicating his prominence (Matt 10:2; Mark 3:16; Luke 6:14; Acts 1:13).
- He was one of the three "inner circle" of disciples; the other two were James and John (Mark 5:37; 9:2; 13:3; 14:33).

- He figures in many of the events in the life of Jesus. He is the one who confessed Jesus as the Son of God (Matt 16:13–20).
- As Jesus had predicted, he denied Jesus at the time of Jesus's death (Matt 26:69–75).
- He was the subject of special attention by Jesus after the resurrection (John 21; see especially verses 15ff).
- He was the one who led the apostles in selecting someone to take Judas's place (Acts 1:15).
- He preached the first gospel sermon in Acts (Acts 2).
- He figures prominently in Acts after that. He also was the first to preach to Gentiles (See, e.g., Acts 3:1–26; 4:8ff; 5:3ff; 8:14ff; 10:1ff; 15:7ff; et al.).
- He later was rebuked by Paul because of his behavior at Antioch (Gal 2:11).
- Apparently, he performed an itinerant ministry (1 Cor 9:5; 1 Cor 1:12; 1 Pet 5:13).
- He wrote the two epistles of Peter.
- According to tradition, he was martyred in Rome by Nero.

B. First Readers: "To the exiles of the Dispersion in Pontus, Galatia, Cappadocia, Asia, and Bithynia ..." (1:1).

- The places named are provinces in Asia Minor or modern Turkey.

- It has been thought that the letter was addressed to Christian Jews in the designated area since it was Jews who were the "Dispersion."
- But it seems unlikely that Peter would say of those who were Jews what he says of the readers in 1:14; 1:18; 2:10; 4:3, 4.
- Furthermore, Peter says that these Christians are now what Israel was in Old Testament times (2:9, 10).
- Thus, it seems most likely that the letter was simply addressed to Christians, and that probably the majority of those who first read it were Gentiles.

C. Provenance: From where was the epistle written? Peter specifies "Babylon" (1 Pet 5:13).

- It seems unlikely this was literal Babylon. See *CMM*, 424.
- It seems more likely that "Babylon" was a code word for "Rome," as it was in Revelation. This would have been a likely place to have written about persecution and suffering and there is a strong tradition that Peter spent time in Rome before his death.

D. Date: When was the letter written?

1. The letter speaks of persecution and suffering because of persecution. 1 Peter 4:16 — "If any man suffer as a Christian ..." Because of this tact, some have thought that it refers to one of the major empire-wide persecutions, such as that

under Domitian in the 90s. That would eliminate Peter as the author.

2. Another persecution was initiated by Nero in the middle 60s. However, there is no evidence that this persecution was empire-wide, so it would not necessarily have affected Christians in Asia Minor.

3. Most recently it has been recognized that the persecution spoken of in 1 Peter is not necessarily one of the major empire-wide persecutions.

(1) It does not, for instance, speak of Christians' losing their lives for the faith. Notice:

- 2:12
- 2:13–15
- 3:13, 14
- 3:16
- 4:1, 2
- 4:12–16

(2) Thus, it has been argued that the persecution spoken of in 1 Peter, and the consequent sufferings, reflect the situation that is found in the book of Acts. Persecution could break out anywhere at any time; Christians needed to be prepared for it.

4. The major persecutions need not, therefore, be the determining factor regarding the time of the epistle. Peter is generally thought to have been killed under Nero, so it seems likely that the letter was written sometime between the date of Paul's letter to the Romans and Peter's death. House (16, 17) gives the date as 63.

E. Message

- The message relates to persecution and suffering; it was intended to help Christians in a time of persecution.
- Black (class notes) says its purpose is "to encourage Christians in Northern Asia Minor who are trying to remain faithful in the face of suffering."

F. Outline (from David and Michaels, as given by Black, class notes)

- Greeting (1:1, 2)
- Foundational themes of the Christian life (1:3–2:10)
- Relating to society's institutions (2:11–4:11)
- Coming to grips with Christian suffering (4:12–5:11)
- Concluding remarks (5:12–14)

2 PETER

A. Authorship and Canonicity

1. The letter claims to be by Peter: "Simeon Peter, a servant and apostle of Jesus Christ" (1:1).

2. Arguments against Peter's authorship, with answers (from Black, class notes):

a. Tradition in favor of Peter's authorship is weak. See below.

b. Stylistic or language differences from 1 Peter. This was noticed by Jerome. In reply: Peter's use of an amanuensis—of Silvanus, 1 Peter 5:12—could explain it.

c. Indications in the book of a late date:

- "Ever since our fathers fell asleep" (2 Peter 3:4) sounds as if the book were written later than Peter's time if, in fact, it is talking about Christians. But it may be that he is talking about the "fathers" of the Old Testament. NRSV: "Ever since our ancestors died."
- The reference to Paul's writings as "scripture" (2 Peter 3:15, 16) suggests a later date to some. But it may rather indicate an earlier date for the recognition of New Testament writings as scripture.
- The letter opposes Gnosticism when it says, "For we did not follow cleverly devised myths." This would make it considerably later. But this expression does not prove the presence of even protognosticism, much less full-blown gnosticism.

d. The use of Jude in 2 Peter 2. But this does not prove that 2 Peter is late, since Jude may be quite early.

e. 2 Peter is theologically different from 1 Peter. This may be so, but it does not contradict 1 Peter.

f. Reflects a Hellenistic background. It uses, e.g., a word for "moral excellence" as the Greeks would have used it. But Peter could have encountered Hellenistic culture.

3. 2 Peter is the least widely attested of all New Testament books. No other New Testament book is so late and doubted.

- The earliest attestation: It was probably used by the writer of the Apocalypse of Peter in the 1st half of the 2nd century.
- There are several 2nd-century allusions.
- Eusebius says Clement of Alexandria wrote a commentary on all the general epistles, which would have included 2 Peter.
- First direct reference to 2 Peter is by Origen, who regarded it as doubted.
- Eusebius lists it among the disputed books.
- Jerome also notes that it is disputed by many, but he accepts it.

4. Arguments in favor of Peter's authorship, from Harrison, 423–425:

a. Various details in the book—e.g., the writer's use of the name Simon Peter, the personal allusions in 1:12–18, the style (as compared with Peter's speeches in Acts and with 1 Peter)—suggest, or are at least consistent with, Petrine authorship.

b. "The alternative to authenticity is pseudonymity."

- But there is no indication that the churches accepted works that they knew to be pseudepigraphical.
- To say the least, it is hard to imagine believing in the inspiration of a book if one cannot accept what the book says about its own authorship.
- Furthermore, since the book teaches only orthodox doctrine, there would be no motive for

someone to write it and then publish it under Peter's name. (*CMM*, 437).

5. Because of the doubts about authorship (see above), the book was accepted into the canon at a relatively late date. It is listed by Athanasius in his festal letter of 367, and after that "it seems to have been generally accepted" (*CMM*, 440).

B. Date and Provenance.

- If Peter is the author, then the book was probably written near the end of his life ("I know that my death will come soon," 2 Pet 1:14, NRSV), most likely sometime in the range 64–68.
- If the book was written by Peter, then Rome would be the most likely place of writing since there is a strong tradition that Peter was there towards the end of his life. (*CMM*, 438) The book itself gives no clues as to where the author was when he wrote the letter.

C. Addressees.

1. The address is very general: "To those who have received a faith as precious as ours through the righteousness of our God and Savior Jesus Christ" (1:1). In this sense, it certainly deserves to be called a "general" or "catholic" epistle.

2. Peter says that this is the "second letter" he has written to the same people (3:1). It is usually thought that the "first letter" was First Peter. If so, then the recipients would have

been "the exiles of the Dispersion in Pontus, Galatia, Cappadocia, Asia, and Bithynia" (2 Pet 1:1).

3. There may be a problem with this view, however, since in 2 Peter 3:1 the writer says that in the first letter, he reminded them that they should "remember the words spoken in the past by the holy prophets, and the commandment of the Lord and Savior spoken through your apostles" (2 Peter 3:2). This does not sound particularly like the epistle of 1 Peter, especially since the writer in 2 Peter 3 goes on to talk about the second coming of Christ as if that was the specific teaching he had written about in his first letter. See Edwin A. Blum, "2 Peter," in *The Expositor's Bible Commentary*, vol. 12, 283, 284.

4. Consequently, if the "first letter" was 1 Peter, we know who the recipients were; if not, we don't, except that we know that they were Christians and were "probably Gentiles" (Harrison, 426).

A. 2 Peter and Jude.

1. The relationship between 2 Peter and Jude presents a special problem since 2 Peter 2 is very similar to Jude: "Most of Jude is included in 2 Peter, no less than nineteen of his twenty-five verses being represented in the longer writing" (*CMM*, 439).

2. It is difficult to say for sure how the two chapters are related.

a. The similarity in wording suggests a literary relationship. But it may not be as close as it at first appears; see *CMM*, 437, where Guthrie is cited.

b. Assuming there was such a relationship, what was it?

- Peter might have used Jude. This is the usual position.
- Jude might have used Peter. This is the position taken by J. W. Roberts, who cites evidence that Peter warned of the coming of false teachers and that Jude referred to those warnings in Jude 17, 18. In 2 Peter 2, the false teachers are in the future ("there will be false teachers among you," 2:1); in Jude, they are already present ("certain intruders have stolen in among you," v. 4). J. W. Roberts, *I and II Peter and Jude* (Austin, TX: R. B. Sweet Co., 1964), 63, 64.
- Both might have used a common source.

c. There is no way to know for sure, but the conclusion one reaches does not necessarily affect one's interpretation of either book nor does it necessarily reflect a negative view of inspiration.

Contents.

1. 2 Peter is largely about false teachers and false teachings. Such teachers are mentioned in every part of the letter:

- "You ... are established in the truth that has come to you" (1:12).
- "We did not follow cleverly devised myths ..." (1:16).
- "There will be false teachers among you (2:1). (See all of chapter 2.)
- "In the last days scoffers will come ..." (3:3).

- Some things in Paul's letters are "... hard to understand, which the ignorant and unstable twist to their own destruction" (3:16).
- "Beware that you are not carried away with the error of the lawless" (3:17).

2. What do we know about these false teachers?

a. What were they like?

(1) They were Christians; they had been "bought" by Christ (2:1).

(2) They were motivated by greed (2:3, 14, 15).

(3) They were licentious, with "eyes full of adultery" (2:2, 10, 14).

(4) They were bold, reveling "in the daytime" (2:10, 13).

(5) They slandered what they did not understand (2:12).

(6) They worked in a way designed to accomplish their aims:

- They "secretly" brought in destructive opinions (2:1).
- They "exploited" Christians and "enticed" new Christians (2:18). E.g., they promised freedom, but could not deliver on the promise (2:19).
- They questioned authority (1:16; 2:1, 10, 11).
- They cited, but misused, scripture (3:16, 17).
- Ultimately, they openly and brazenly taught and acted according to their false teaching (2:13).

(7) The result of their lives and teaching was that "the way of truth" was "maligned" (2:2).

b. What did they teach?

- They apparently taught that the apostles had taught "cleverly devised myths" about Jesus Christ (1:16).
- They taught "destructive opinions," "bombastic nonsense" (2:1, 18).
- They will "deny the Master who bought them" (2:2).
- They indulge the flesh and use "licentious desires" to entice people (2:10, 18).
- They despised authority (2:10).
- They denied that Christ would come again (3:3, 4).

c. What would be their end? (2:3, 4–10, 12-13, 17, 20–22)

3. It's interesting to compare 1 Peter and 2 Peter. Both are about problems facing the church.

- 1 Peter: Problems from without—the suffering that comes from persecution. Tenney calls his chapter on 1 Peter "The Suffering Church" and his outline on 1 Peter is headed "Salvation Through Suffering." Merrill C. Tenney, *The New Testament: An Historical and Analytic Survey* (Grand Rapids, MI: Eerdmans, 1955), 359, 365.
- 2 Peter: Problems from within—the problems caused by false teachers. Tenney includes 2 Peter along with Jude and the epistles of John in a chapter he calls "The Peril of Heresies" (Tenney, 383ff).

4. Purpose and outline

a. Perhaps the purpose of the letter is best expressed in its last two verses: "Since you are forewarned, beware that you are not carried away with the error of the lawless and lose your own stability. But grow in the grace and knowledge of our Lord and Savior Jesus Christ" (3:17, 18). The twofold aim: (1) Don't be led astray by false teachers. (2) To avoid this, do grow in the Lord.

b. Outline: Following the introductory verses (1:1, 2) the letter can be seen as a means to accomplish this objective: In order that this purpose may be achieved ...

- You need to know how and why to grow (1:3–11).
- You need to know the certainty of what you have believed (1:12–21).
- You need to know about the false teachers (2:1–22).
- You need to know about the second coming which the false teachers deny (3:1–16).
- You need to be reminded of your most important immediate spiritual need(s) (3:17, 18).

Notes on 1, 2, and 3 John

TYPE OF WRITING

A. First John is classified as a "general epistle." It deserves the name from the standpoint that it says nothing specific about having been written to a particular church or group of churches.

B. However, it lacks several characteristics of a letter. For example, it neither begins nor ends like a letter. Nevertheless, Carson, Moo, and Morris insist that it is a letter, not, e.g., an "abstract paper, a mere brochure, or a tractate for all Christians everywhere" (445).

CANONICITY

First John apparently enjoyed greater acceptance and circulation earlier than did many of the other general epistles.

AUTHOR AND PROVENANCE

A. There is evidence that John the apostle, the author of the gospel of John, is also the author of 1 John.

- There is considerable external evidence for John's authorship of 1 John. According to Eusebius, Papias used First John. Irenaeus, Clement of Alexandria, Tertullian, and the Muratorian canon all credit the epistle to John (Black, 45).
- "The vocabulary, style, and concepts in the epistles and the Gospel are similar and suggest common authorship" (Black, 45; see *CMM*, 447).

B. The major alternative to John's authorship is the idea that a "Johannine community" authored the book(s).

- For example, the introduction to 1 John in the *Oxford Annotated Bible* says, "Although traditionally called a letter, 1 John is a treatise or sermon from an unknown teacher in the Johannine tradition to those in the community."
- There is insufficient evidence to reject the traditional view of authorship in favor of an "unknown teacher." *CMM* indicate that the biggest problem with this approach to the Johannine literature is the piling up of "merely possible inferences." (*CMM*, 457).

C. The most likely place of writing for all three of John's letters is Ephesus, where John apparently spent his last years. (*CMM*, 450).

DATE

Usually, 1 John is dated after the gospel of John, but there is no good reason to conclude that one is earlier than the other. Most suggest 1 John was written about 85–95. House dates all the epistles of John in the "late 80s or early 90s" in *Chronological and Background Charts of the New Testament*, 17.

ADDRESSEES

A. Obviously, the letter was written to Christians.

B. It seems equally obvious that these were Christians who were bothered by false teachers and teachings. See below.

C. Beyond that, it is not possible to say to whom the book was addressed since the book itself gives no indication of the area in which the readers lived. Black suggests that it might have been written to a local church or to a regional group of churches troubled by false teachers, usually thought to be near Ephesus, but that probably it was not written to the whole Christian brotherhood (*An Outline of New Testament Introduction*, 46, and Class Notes.)

MESSAGE

A. First John is hard to outline.

B. It is also hard to say what is its primary theme or principal message. Rather than there being one overriding theme, there seem to be several different emphases.

- The correct teaching about Jesus Christ, the Son of God
- Love
- Knowing
- Not sinning, not being "of the world"
- Fellowship

C. 1. John speaks of several purposes his letter is designed to achieve. Consider the following passages (there are others in which John says, "I am writing to you because ...," but those passages do not seem to represent the purpose John has in mind).

- 1:1–3 — "We declare to you what we have seen and heard so that you also may have fellowship with us ..." (v.3)
- 1:4 — "We are writing these things so that our joy may be complete."
- 2:1 — "I am writing these things to you so that you may not sin."
- 5:13 — "I write these things to you who believe in the name of the Son of God, so that you may know that you have eternal life."

2. These purposes do not seem to be contradictory, but to be supplementary. According to these passages, John wrote for two reasons, with two anticipated results:

a. He wrote so that his readers could know with certainty what John knew, in order that they might have fellowship with John and other Christians, which meant they would also have fellowship with God and Christ.

b. The result of the acceptance of this knowledge would be the completion of John's joy.

c. He also wrote so that they might not sin.

d. If they accepted and lived by the correct understanding of the person of Christ and the inadmissibility of sin in the Christian's life, the anticipated result would be the assurance that they had eternal life.

e. This twofold emphasis—believing that Jesus is the Christ, the Son of God, and living a life consistent with that belief—is found in several places in the letter:

- "This is his commandment, that we should believe in the name of his Son Jesus Christ and love one another ..." (3:23).
- "We know that those who are born of God do not sin ... that we are God's children ... that the Son of God has come and has given us understanding so that we may know him who is true; and we are in him who is true, in his Son Jesus Christ. He is the true God and eternal life" (5:18–20).

D. To expand on these ideas, here is a possible re-

creation of the situation John faced and the purpose(s) he
hoped to achieve.

1. Some false teachers were spreading a brand of an
early kind of Gnosticism (proto-Gnosticism). Gnosticism
taught that spirit was good and matter—anything material,
including flesh—was bad.

2. As part of their program, they taught that Jesus could
not have been really God and truly man at the same time;
they, therefore, denied His real manhood (since the physical
is evil, God could not become flesh). This might have been a
kind of Docetism, which taught that the Son of God was not
truly flesh, but only "seemed" to be so.

- 2:22, 23 — "Who is the liar but the one who
  denies that Jesus is the Christ?" (v.22)
- 3:15 — "God abides in those who confess that
  Jesus is the Son of God, and they abide in God."
- 4:1–6 — "By this you know the Spirit of God:
  every spirit that confesses that Jesus Christ has
  come in the flesh is from God" (v.2).
- 5:1 — "Everyone who believes that Jesus is the
  Christ has been born of God." (See also 5:5—12;
  5:20, 21.)

3. They also apparently asserted that it was possible to
be a Christian without leading a life of purity, obedience,
and love. One conclusion reached by Gnostics was that a
man's spiritual life was not affected by his behavior in the
physical world.

- This would help us understand such passages as: 1:5–10; 2:3–6; 2:15–17; 2:29; 3:3–10; 3:24; 5:17, 18.
- It may be that these false teachers also made necessary the emphasis in the letter on "love." Perhaps they acted unlovingly. Perhaps their teaching that how you live makes no difference in your relationship with God led them to discredit the importance of love. Whatever the reason, the emphasis in the book on loving one another is obvious. See: 2:9–11; 3:11–23; 4:7–21.

4. They may have claimed that their teachings were part of the special knowledge that only they possessed. They alone were the "knowing" ones. (The word "Gnosticism" comes from a Greek word for "knowing.")

5. This superior attitude might then have created confusion and a feeling of inferiority on the part of the Christians to whom John wrote. *CMM*: "They were being made to feel inferior and spiritually threatened" (452).

6. Along with the false teachers' view that they alone were knowledgeable, their teachings that (a) Jesus was not really both God and man and (b) it makes no difference how you live, would have led Christians into great uncertainty. Could they know for sure what was true? Whether Jesus Christ was God and man? Whether it was possible to go to heaven without the "special knowledge" of the proto-Gnostics?

7. John wrote to tell them: Yes, it is possible to know, to be sure of the truths you have learned, and to be sure that

you can go to heaven! John emphasizes what Christians can *know*. The word "know" (translated from two different Greek words) is found in the RSV 34 times in 1 John (and in the KJV 26 times).

8. Thus, it is possible to say that the theme of 1 John is "Assurance."

- "Now by this we may be sure that we know him, if we obey his commandments" (2:3).
- "If what you have heard from the beginning abides in you, then you will abide in the Son and in the Father" (2:24b).
- "We know that we have passed from death to life because we love one another"(3:14). "Let us love, not in word or speech, but in truth and action. And by this we will know that we are from the truth and will reassure our hearts before him" (3:18, 19; See also: 4:7, 8, 12).
- "By this we know that he abides in us, by the Spirit that he has given us" (3:24b; See also: 4:13).
- "By this we know that we love the children of God, when we love God and obey his commandments" (5:2).
- "I write these things to you who believe in the name of the Son of God, so that you may know that you have eternal life" (5:13).

PROBLEM PASSAGE(S)

A. Perhaps the most difficult problem presented by the content of 1 John is contained in the messages of 3:6, 8, 9, 10, and 5:18. All of these verses seem to say it is impossible for the Christian to sin.

B. Yet this would apparently contradict (1) other New Testament passages and (2) other verses in 1 John itself—see 1:8, 10.

C. The solution to this apparent contradiction probably lies in the fact that the words used for "sinning" in the passages cited above are in the present tense, which is a continuing tense. They, therefore, mean something like: He who is truly a Christian does not keep on sinning.

TEXTUAL ISSUE

A. In the KJV, 1 John includes the words: "There are three that bear record in heaven, the Father, the Word, and the Holy Ghost: and these three are one" (5:7). These words are left out of more recent versions.

B. In this case, there is little doubt about the manuscript evidence. There is no support in the ancient manuscripts for the KJV reading. See *CMM*, 455.

2 and 3 John

INTRODUCTION

I. 2 and 3 John share with Philemon and Jude the distinction of being New Testament books with only one chapter each.

II. There is no way to know in what order John's epistles were written.

III. In contrast to 1 John, both 2 and 3 John are very obvious letters. They include an opening and a closing and were intended to deal with very specific problems.

CANONICITY

A. Both these letters were among the books classified by Eusebius as "disputed." They were, however, accepted by all by the middle of the fourth century.

B. It is possible that their brevity—and perhaps their relative lack of theological significance—contributed to the slowness of their acceptance.

AUTHOR

A. 2 and 3 John are linked to 1 John by vocabulary and theme (*CMM*, 449) and John's gospel and epistles are tied together by their vocabulary, style, and concepts (Black, 45).

B. Both 2 and 3 John are written by "the elder" who does not identify himself further. This does not point to someone other than John as the writer, since an apostle could also be an elder (see 1 Pet 5:1). It may emphasize the fact of John's advancing years or maybe another way of asserting his authority.

CONTENTS

A. 2 John.

- 2 John is addressed to "the elect lady and her children" (v. 1). It is usually thought that this refers to a local congregation.
- It was written to combat the same kind of false teaching that is dealt with in 1 John: "Many deceivers have gone out in the world, those who do not confess that Jesus Christ has come in the flesh; such a person is the deceiver and the antichrist!" (v. 7) (Compare 1 John 2:18, 22.)
- Specifically, those who are addressed in this letter are told not to have any fellowship with these false teachers: "Do not receive in the house or welcome anyone who comes to you and does not bring this teaching" (v. 10; see vv. 9—11).

B. 3 John.

- 3 John is addressed to "the beloved Gaius" (v. 1).
- It was written to encourage Gaius (and others) to continue to receive and support faithful evangelists (which would probably include Demetrius) (vv. 5–8, 12).
- In contrast, Diotrephes refused to receive such evangelists, especially since they, or when they, carried authoritative letters from the elder. Diotrephes is warned that John will deal with him (vv. 9, 10).

Conclusion

I. In general, the letters of John, like the letters of 2 Peter and Jude, remind us of how important it was and is to hold to the truth "once for all delivered to the saints."

II. One of my students pointed out that the message of the three epistles of John might be summed up in the word "fellowship."

- 1 John: We need to have fellowship with God.
- 2 John: We must not have fellowship with error.
- 3 John: We should have fellowship with God's messengers.

Notes on Jude

INTRODUCTION

JUDE IS ONE OF THE FOUR ONE-CHAPTER BOOKS OF THE New Testament. The others are Philemon and 2 and 3 John.

AUTHOR AND DATE

A. The author identifies himself as "Jude, a servant of Jesus Christ and brother of James" (v. 1).

B. It is usually thought that this Jude was one of the brothers of Jesus (Mark 6:3; Matt 13:55) since he identifies himself as the brother of James and James, the Lord's brother, is the only James well enough known in the early church to be identified by his name alone (Carson, Moo, and Morris, 459). (See notes on the book of James.) There are other men named "Jude" in the New Testament (Luke 6:16; Acts 1:13; John 14:22), but there is no reason to suppose that any one of them is the author (*CMM*, 460).

C. There is little in the letter to indicate when the letter was written. House dates the book in the 60s or 70s (*Chronological and Background Charts of the New Testament*, 17) and Guthrie between 65 and 80 (Cited in *CMM*, 460).

RECIPIENTS

A. The letter's intended audience is very general; it is addressed to "those who are called, who are beloved in God the Father and kept safe for Jesus Christ" (v. 1).

B. Beyond that, we can know that Jude was speaking to Christians: they were called (v. 1) and they shared salvation with him (v. 3).

C. It is likely also that they were Jews since Jude uses Jewish apocryphal writings in the letter.

D. He may have a particular congregation in mind since he speaks of them in endearing terms (v. 3) and uses the second person pronoun when he says that false teachers had slipped in among them (v. 3). If so, there is no way to know where it was (*CMM*, 460).

OCCASION

A. Jude had intended to write about their "common salvation" (v. 3, KJV).

B. Instead, he felt obligated to write to warn them about false teachers, "certain intruders" who "have stolen in among you," people who "pervert the grace of our God into licentiousness and deny" Christ. (v. 4)

CRITICAL ISSUES

A. Canonicity. According to *CMM* (461):

1. Traces of the letter in Clement of Rome, Hermas, Polycarp, Barnabas, and perhaps the Didache, but not definitely cited as Scripture.

2. Mentioned in the Muratorian Canon.

3. Cited by such writers as Tertullian and Clement of Alexandria.

4. Used by Origen, who implies that others did not accept it.

5. Accepted by Eusebius, but placed among the disputed books.

6. Eventually accepted by all.

7. Doubts arose because of:

- a. Its use of apocryphal books.
- b. Its brevity.

B. Relationship to 2 Peter. Jude and 2 Peter 2 are very much alike. There seems to be a literary relationship between them. It is impossible to know with certainty what that relationship is. See notes on 2 Peter.

C. Quotations from pseudepigraphical works.

1. The writer quotes from *The Assumption of Moses* (v. 9) and the *Apocalypse of Enoch* (v. 14). (Even though the story about Michael is cited by Origen, Clement, and Didymus as coming from *The Assumption of Moses*, we don't have the story in the copies of the *Assumption* that have come down to the present day.)

2. How shall we regard such a fact?

a. It caused some early Christians to reject the book as canonical.

b. Tertullian used Jude's quotation from Enoch to prove the canonicity of 1 Enoch. 1 Enoch 1:9 is quoted word-for-word in Jude (Black, class notes, spring, 1994).

c. Harrison notes that "one method of circumventing the difficulty is to assert that Jude's citation is simply an appeal to tradition regarded as coming down from the patriarch [Enoch] himself. This is improbable ..." (Harrison, 431).

d. The more common approach today by conservatives is to assume that Jude cites or quotes these works, not as inspired scripture, but as books and stories that were well known and accepted by the audience to which he was speaking, much as Paul quoted pagan poets and philosophers (Acts 17:28; 1 Cor 15:33; Titus 1:12). See Harrison, 431.

(1) Is this less likely since Jude says that Enoch "prophesied" (v. 14), using a word that generally speaks of God's inspiration?

(2) Not necessarily, since Paul, in Titus 1:12, speaks of one of the Cretans, "their very own prophet," without quoting from an inspired book.

CONTENT

A. The book is given over largely to a condemnation of these false teachers. Their teaching apparently featured a kind of antinomianism (against the law):

- Advocating the freedom to indulge in immorality —see vv.4, 7, 8, 16, 18, 19.

- Denying and even actively attacking constituted authority—see vv. 4, 6, 8–10.

B. The solution to the problem posed by the false teachers was:

- "Contend for the faith ..." v. 3
- "Build yourselves up ..." v. 20
- "Pray in the Holy Spirit" v. 20
- "Keep yourselves in the love of God" v. 21
- "Look forward to the mercy of our Lord ... which leads to eternal life" v.21
- Be concerned about and help save others. vv. 22, 23
- Recognize that God "is able to keep you from falling ..." vv. 24, 25

C. The book ends with a doxology (vv. 24, 25). This is unusual for New Testament letters; only 2 Peter (to a small extent) and Romans share this characteristic.

D. Purpose

1. The primary purpose of the book is given by Jude himself: He writes it to urge his readers to "contend for the faith that was once for all entrusted to the saints" (v. 3).

2. Its secondary purpose is to contribute to its readers keeping themselves, keeping others, and being kept (vv. 21–24) in the faith.

E. Outline (from *Harper Study Bible*):

- Introduction (1–4)
- Character and doom of false teachers (5–16)

- Admonition to hold the true faith (17–23)
- Benediction (24, 25)

Notes on Revelation

TITLE

A. WHERE DOES THE BOOK GET ITS TITLE? FROM THE first words of the text, the very first word of the Greek text: *Apokalupsis*; transliterated "apocalypse;" when you read about the "Apocalypse," you are simply reading about Revelation. This Greek word means an uncovering or unveiling.

B. The book is the "Revelation of Jesus Christ," not the "Revelation of John." Notice it is "Revelation" [singular], not "Revelations" [plural].

AUTHOR

A. The author claims to be John (1:1, 2) who writes because God has shown him a vision while he is on the island of Patmos (1:9–11). Traditionally, authorship has been ascribed to John the apostle, who also wrote the gospel of John and the three epistles of John.

B. External evidence for this view dates from the second and third centuries. "No New Testament book ... has a stronger or earlier tradition about its authorship than does Revelation." (Carson, Moo, and Morris, 468).

C. But the idea that Revelation was written by John the apostle was questioned by Dionysius, a third-century bishop of Alexandria. Apparently, he did not like the book because it seemed to him to teach a thousand-year reign of Christ on earth (called chiliasm then, premillennialism now). Because of Dionysius, the canonicity of Revelation was often questioned during the years that followed.

D. The arguments against John's authorship are all internal and are the same today as those used by Dionysius. Those arguments are given below, as they are found in *CMM* (469–472), along with answers.

1. The author cannot be an apostle because he never claims to be, never alludes to gospel events, and never claims a special relationship with Christ, but credits the apostles with too much authority (see 18:20 and 21:14).

- Answer one: It is not the purpose of the book to deal with Jesus's life on earth; therefore, the apostle John's relationship to the Lord is not relevant to the communication.
- Answer two: John places no more emphasis on the apostles than Paul (Eph 2:20) or Jesus (Matt 16:17–19).

2. The author cannot be the person who wrote the gospel of John and the epistles because the theology—involving theology proper, Christology, and eschatology—of

Revelation is different from "the theology of the fourth gospel and of 1 John" (*CMM*, 470).

- For example, in Revelation God is a "God of majesty and judgment, while the God of the gospel and epistles is a God of love" (*CMM*, 470).
- Answer one: While the difference may be admitted, it does not prove that the writings are from different hands. The message is complementary, not contradictory. Only a preconceived notion of what God is or must be would fail to acknowledge that possibility.
- Answer two: "The contrasts are ... overdrawn ... . Both the gospel and Revelation teach that God is *both* loving and judging, that Christ is *both* redeemer and sovereign Lord ..." (*CMM*, 470).
- Answer three: There are many similarities among the writings.

3. There are considerable differences between the Greek of Revelation and that of John's other writings. *CMM* quotes Charles as saying, "The Greek of Revelation is 'unlike any Greek that was ever penned by mortal man'" (*CMM*, 470). This is the most important argument; great differences exist. Some possible explanations:

- A difference in time between Revelation and John's other writings. But this does not seem likely (*CMM*, 471).

- A difference in amanuensis, or the lack of an amanuensis when John wrote Revelation.
- Revelation was deliberately written that way, for one of several reasons.
- [A difference in subject matter.]
- There are also similarities in style.

E. The alternatives to John's authorship are untenable.

1. It was not likely written by John the Baptist or by John Mark.

2. It is thought that Papias mentions a "John the elder" who is different from "John the apostle." However, it is not clear in the passage that is cited that he is talking about two different people.

3. The idea that it was written by a "Johannine community" or "circle" is an unproved and unprovable hypothesis, but nothing more.

4. The idea that it was written by someone who published the writing pseudonymously is unlikely, especially since external evidence credits the book to John and evidence is lacking that the church knowingly accepted pseudonymous literature.

5. The only other alternative is that a John who is unknown to us, but was known at the end of the first century, wrote the book. But this does not seem more likely than that the apostle John, who was undoubtedly well known, was its author.

6. Thus, there is no likely alternative to the view that Revelation was written by John the apostle.

WHEN, FROM WHERE, TO WHOM WRITTEN

A. From where written? Island of Patmos (1:9).

   B. About when? Perhaps about AD95, during the reign of Domitian. See the discussion in *CMM*, 473–476.

   C. To whom? Seven churches of Asia. But these were not the only intended audience: "he who has an ear, let him hear what the Spirit says to the churches" implies a broader audience than "the seven churches."

CIRCUMSTANCES OF WRITING, THEME

A. A time of persecution: Christians were dying for the faith (6:9, 10).

   B. The theme or main idea of the book is God wins—in the end.

   C. How would this theme have met the needs of the people for whom it was written? In spite of the present circumstances, when evil seems to be winning, when the devil has the upper hand, in the end, the forces of God and of good will prevail; therefore, Christians can take heart! God's people will be on the winning side, and, if they remain faithful in spite of persecution, they can and will be saved!

KIND OF LITERATURE, OR GENRE

A. Revelation is three kinds of literature: epistle, apocalyptic, and prophecy (*CMM*, 478).

   B. Apocalyptic:

- This was a very popular kind of literature among the Jews from about 200 BC to about AD 200.
- Characteristics: One source says: Its primary characteristics are that it is [1) dualistic, and [2] eschatological. Its secondary characteristics are that it [1] is visionary, [2] is messianic, [3] emphasizes angelology and demonology, [4] uses animal symbolism, [5] uses numerology, [6] includes the prediction of woes, [7] features the final triumph of light over darkness.
- From a consideration of Jewish apocalypses, it is sometimes said that one characteristic of this genre is that the books are pseudonymous. If so, the book of Revelation does not fit in the category (*CMM*, 479). (For this and other reasons, *CMM* say they are "reluctant to consider Revelation an apocalypse" *CMM*, 479).
- The book of Daniel and parts of Ezekiel and Zechariah are sometimes placed in this genre.
- "Why would John write like that?" (Or why would the Holy Spirit inspire John to write like that?) Both to reveal and to conceal. To some, who had the "key" to the interpretation, it would reveal what the writer intended to say. But it would conceal the truth from others who lacked that "key." It was almost certainly intended to be difficult for some to understand.

C. Revelation is a book of *prophecy* since it deals with the future (4:1).

D. Revelation is also an *epistle*, or at least contains seven letters to churches. See Revelation 2 and 3.

E. *CMM* conclude their discussion of the point: "We may best view Revelation, then, as a prophecy cast in an apocalyptic mold and written down in a letter form" (*CMM*, 479).

INTERPRETATION

A. Four methods or theories of interpretation are identified by Harrison in *Introduction to the Old Testament*, 462–465 (and by *CMM*). For "Interpretations of Revelation" and "Theological Perspectives on Revelation," see also House, 145 (and 146, 147 for the structure and contents of the book).

1. The preterist view—"the great mass of the material must be understood as pertaining to the period in which the book was written." Also called the "contemporary-historical" approach (*CMM*, 482). Virtually everything in the book was fulfilled by the end of the first century: "the visions of John grow out of and describe events in John's own day" (*CMM*, 482).

2. The historicist view—"seeks to interpret the material in terms of church history by identifying various items in the visions with leading movements and events from the apostolic age to modern times." History written in advance: Approximately chapters 5–19 were future at the time of the book's writing and are

now past. *CMM:* "A sketch of history from the time of Christ to [the interpreter's] day" (482).

3. The futurist view—"understands the central chapters as setting forth events of the end-time leading up to the return of Christ and intimately connected therewith." *CMM:* "Holds that everything in the Revelation from chapter 4 to the end finds its fulfillment in the very last days of human history." (483; *CMM* subscribe to the futurist approach.) Sometimes chapters 2 and 3 are believed to depict seven periods of church history.

4. The idealist or spiritual view—maintains "that the apocalyptic dress is merely intended to set forth the ageless struggle between the kingdom of God and the forces of evil arrayed against it." *CMM:* "The symbolism is designed ... to help us understand God's person and ways with the world in a general way, not to enable us to map out a course of events" (483).

B. Three theories concerning the millennium (the thousand years) of which Revelation 20 speaks:

1. Premillennialism—Christ will come before [pre] the millennium.
2. Postmillennialism—the millennium will occur and then Christ will come after [post] the millennium.

3. Amillennialism—there will be no literal thousand-year reign, no [a] millennium.

4. Most members of churches of Christ are amillennial. There may have been a strain of postmillennialism in Alexander Campbell when he called his paper the *Millennial Harbinger*. He may have believed that the spread of the gospel would bring in the millennium—not a literal thousand years, but a period of gospel prosperity.

C. What can we say in general about the interpretation of the book?

- It was intended to be understood, at least by some (1:3).
- In some sense, it was intended to be acted upon (1:3).
- Since those seven churches actually existed, it is most likely that what the Spirit had to say to them is to be taken literally, although this particular seven may have been chosen for a special reason—as exemplars, for instance, of characteristics of others.
- At least some of the things described in the book were future to the people who first received it.
- It is obvious that much of the book is symbolic, written in figurative language, because the book itself in several places explains some of the details of the visions, saying, in effect, "This represents that." Where the book does this,

today's reader can be sure of the meaning of the symbol(s).

- It seems to be axiomatic—see number one above —that what seems so mysterious to us was probably not mysterious to the intended readers, who had clues, who had the "key(s)" to understand the visions and symbols John uses— "key(s)," we do not now possess.
- We should avoid interpreting the book in such a way that it would have made no sense whatsoever to the first readers.
- While Revelation is hard to understand in its details, the main thrust of the message is easy to grasp; it seems likely that anyone reading the book through at one sitting looking for this message would get it. For that message, see under "theme."

CHARACTERISTICS

The following list is from Harrison (460–462).

- It is the biblical book of the end-time par excellence ...
- It is a mysterious book, filled with enigmas for the modern reader. But this does not mean that it was necessarily so for believers who read it at the end of the first century ...
- It is a polemical book, which challenges the pride and impiety of a ruler who claims divine honors, the crowning infamy of paganism ...

- It is a dramatic work. This feature belongs to the nature of apocalyptic in general, but the artistry here is incomparable ...
- A notable element is the interplay between heaven and earth ... Heaven is open to the prophet ...
- There is an emphasis on the unity and godlessness of the nations ...
- Despite its preoccupation with judgment and woe, this book has ample room for worship and praise ...
- Prolific use is made of numbers ...
- Large sections of the text are rhythmical in form ...
- There is frequent use of the Old Testament ... of the 404 verses ... 278 contain references to the Jewish Scriptures ...
- Irregularities in grammar are more common than elsewhere in the New Testament.

Bibliography

BLACK, ALLEN. *AN OUTLINE OF NEW TESTAMENT Introduction*, Memphis, TN: Harding Graduate School of Theology, 1994.

Blum, Edwin A. "2 Peter." Pages 283–84 in vol. 12 of *The Expositor's Bible Commentary*. Edited by Frank E. Gaebelein. Grand Rapids, MI: Zondervan, 1979.

Bruce, F. F. *The New Testament Documents: Are They Reliable?* 5th rev. ed. Grand Rapids, MI: Eerdmans, 1960.

Carson, D. A., Douglas J. Moo, and Leon Morris, *An Introduction to the New Testament*, Grand Rapids, MI: Zondervan, 1992.

Davis, John D. *Dictionary of the Bible*. Grand Rapids: Baker Book House, 1972.

DeHoff, George W. *Alleged Bible Contradictions Explained*. Murfreesboro, TN: DeHoff Publications, 1970.

Geisler, Norman L., and Ronald M. Brooks, *When Skeptics Ask: A Handbook on Christian Evidences*. Wheaton, IL: Victor Books, 1990.

Guthrie, Donald. *New Testament Introduction*. Rev ed. Master Reference Collection. Downers Grove, IL: InterVarsity Press, 1990.

Harrison, Everett F. *Introduction to the New Testament*. New rev. ed. Grand Rapids, MI: Eerdmans, 1971.

Hiebert, D. Edmond. *An Introduction to the Pauline Epistles*. Chicago, IL: Moody Press, 1954.

Holmes, Michael W. "Textual Criticism." Pages 101–134 in *New Testament Criticism and Interpretation: Essays on Methods and Issues*. Edited by David Alan Black and David S. Dockery. Grand Rapids, MI: Zondervan, 1991.

House, H. Wayne. *Chronological and Background Charts of the New Testament*. Grand Rapids, MI: Zondervan, 1981.

Jervell, Jacob. *Luke and the People of God: A New Look at Luke-Acts*. Minneapolis, MN: Augsburg Publishing House, 1972.

Liefeld, Walter L. "Luke." Pages 797–1059 in vol. 8 of *Expositor's Bible Commentary*. Edited by Frank E. Gaebelein. Grand Rapids, MI: Zondervan, 1979.

Lindsell, Harold, ed. *Harper Study Bible*. Grand Rapids, MI: Zondervan, 1952.

May, Herbert G., and Bruce M. Metzger, eds. *The New Oxford Annotated Bible*. New York, NY: Oxford University Press, 1977.

McGarvey, J. W. *Evidences of Christianity*. Nashville, TN: Gospel Advocate Company, 1886.

Metzger, Bruce M. "Colossians." *The New Oxford Annotated Bible Notes*. Edited by Herbert G. May and Bruce M. Metzger. New York, NY: Oxford University Press, 1977.

Roberts, J. W. *I and II Peter and Jude*. Austin, TX: R. B. Sweet Co., 1964.

Smith, William G. *The New Smith's Bible Dictionary*. New York, NY: Doubleday, 1966.

Soulen, Richard N. *Handbook of Biblical Criticism*. 2nd ed. Atlanta, GA: John Knox Press, 1981.

Souter, Alexander and Frederick C. Grant. "Corinth." Pages 176–177 in *Dictionary of the Bible*. Hastings, James, Frederick C. Grant, and H. H. Rowley, eds. New York, NY: Scribner's, 1963.

Tenney, Merrill C. *The New Testament: An Historical and Analytic Survey*. Grand Rapids, MI: Eerdmans, 1955.

Tenny, Merrill C. *New Testament Survey*. Grand Rapids, MI: Eerdmans, 1961.

Weed, Michael R. *The Letters of Paul to the Ephesians, Colossians, and Philemon*. The Living Word Commentary. Austin, TX: Sweet Publishing, 1971.

Williams, Joel Stephen. "Textual Criticism and Bible Translations." *Gospel Light* 63.12 (1993): 184–85.

Wilson, Richard F. "General Letters." Page 320 in *Mercer Dictionary of the Bible*. Edited by Watson E. Miles. Atlanta, GA: Mercer University Press, 1990.

Also by Cypress Publications

The Old Testament: A Study Guide by Coy D. Roper

Ecclesiastes: A Document Designed to Disturb by Coy D. Roper

Approaching Christian Scriptures Faithfully: Twenty Attempts by Ed Gallagher

The Christian Life: Chapters for Bible Teachers by Ed Gallagher

Cruciform Christ: 52 Reflection on the Gospel of Mark by Travis Bookout

Imperative: Studies from the Book of James by Ismael Berlanga

Jesus the Christ: Chapters for Bible Teachers by Ed Gallagher

King of Glory: 52 Reflections on the Gospel of John by Travis Bookout

The Magnitude of God: Exploring the Divine by Brian Poe

Rescue: God and Sin in the Old Testament by John F. Wakefield

Romans: A Practical Commentary by Brian Poe

Visions of Restoration: The History of Churches of Christ by John Young

Women in the Shadows by Betty Hamblen

An Imprint of Heritage Christian University Press

To see full catalog of Heritage Christian University Press
and its imprint Cypress Publications, visit
www.hcu.edu/publications

Milton Keynes UK
Ingram Content Group UK Ltd.
UKHW010212010524
442030UK00003B/48